A Frontier Lady

RECOLLECTIONS OF THE GOLD RUSH

AND EARLY CALIFORNIA

By Sarah Royce

WITH A FOREWORD BY KATHARINE ROYCE

EDITED BY

Ralph Henry Gabriel

University of Nebraska Press

LINCOLN AND LONDON

Publishers on the Plains

UNP

First Bison Book printing: 1977

Most recent printing indicated by first digit below:
1   2   3   4   5   6   7   8   9   10

Library of Congress Cataloging in Publication Data

Royce, Sarah Bayliss.
    A frontier lady.

    "A Bison book."
    Reprint of the 1932 ed. published by Yale Univer-
sity Press, New Haven.
    1. California—Gold discoveries. 2 Overland jour-
nies to the Pacific. 3. Frontier and pioneer life—Cali-
fornia. 4. Pioneers—California—Biography. 5. Royce,
Sarah Bayliss. I. Title.
F865.R86 1977   979.4 [B]   76-44263
ISBN 0-8032-0909-6
ISBN 0-8032-5856-9 pbk.

Bison Book edition reprinted by arrangement with
Yale University Press.

Manufactured in the United States of America

Foreword

MANY years ago, my husband, Professor Josiah Royce of Harvard University, asked his mother if she could thread together and shape as a continuous narrative, for his pleasure and instruction, her old "Pilgrimage Diary." This she gladly did, for the purpose of interesting and pleasing her only son, and of course without any thought of publication; for this reason the following story of the Westward Journey in '49 and of early California days and ways, is completely straightforward and sincere as well as vivid. Some younger readers might easily feel the careful, old-style expressions to be a trifle elaborate. But older readers will realize that the mode of expression was customary and perfectly natural for the people of that earlier time.

I feel sure that Mrs. Royce's devout and unfailing religious belief stood by her through all difficulties and dangers and enabled her to keep her courage and to help others to keep theirs, whatever happened.

It has always seemed to me that the unfailing energy and cheerfulness with which Mrs. Royce met all hardships and rude conditions of living were especially fine in her because she dearly prized the benefits of civilization, not the gaieties or luxuries, but the churches, the libraries, the schools, and the companionship of an enlightened society. She was indeed giving up much.

Yet wherever she was, she made civilization, even when it seemed that she had little indeed from which to

[iii]

make it. It is no light matter to leave home and friends and set out with husband and one baby girl for a long and dangerous journey and to begin a new life in a new land under unknown conditions. But no matter what the surroundings, this brave and persevering woman never roughened nor allowed her children to roughen. In a Sierra Nevada mining camp town she managed to give her four children, of whom Josiah Royce was the youngest, an excellent early training, having for them astronomical charts, histories, and an encyclopedia of common and scientific knowledge and other instructive books.

Possibly it may interest readers to have some further idea of the persons who met with the adventures narrated by Mrs. Royce. Both she and her husband were of English parentage and born in England, but were brought to America in childhood. The writer of the narrative, Sarah Eleanor Bayliss, was born at Stratford on Avon. When she was six weeks old, she was carried on board ship to come to this country at the very moment that the guns were heard celebrating the birth of Queen Victoria. Indeed her whole life was passed during the "Victorian Era."

She was brought up in New York State, and had a careful, old-style academy education, supplemented throughout her life by much reading and study. In her day the range of subjects taught was of course far narrower than now, but the studious were glad to take full advantage of all there was within their reach and so they won a really solid education. It was very characteristic of Mrs. Royce that when bidden at a time of danger to abandon almost all her possessions, she rescued and brought through to California her Bible, her Milton, and a tiny lap writing desk.

Josiah Royce, who took the long journey with his wife, Sarah Eleanor, and their baby Mary, grew up on his father's farm in this country, but left the farm and engaged in various kinds of business. Some years later he had a farm of his own near Grass Valley, California, where his fourth child and only son Josiah, afterward of Harvard, was born and passed his childhood.

KATHARINE ROYCE.

Cambridge, Massachusetts,
  June, 1932.

Concerning the
Manuscript of Sarah Royce

JOSIAH ROYCE was a young lecturer in philosophy at Harvard in the eighteen eighties when he was asked to prepare a history of the early American period in the state of California. The task was a congenial one for Royce had been born in a mining camp in the shadow of the Sierras. He had spent much of his boyhood in an uncouth and dissolute San Francisco which the gold rush had sent sprawling along the shores of the Bay. Royce's parents, moreover, were Forty-niners who had jolted overland across the continent in a covered wagon. In the eighties the young Harvard lecturer was already probably the most distinguished intellectual that frontier California had produced. Royce accepted this invitation to prepare a volume in the "American Commonwealths" series. As part of his collecting for his history he asked his mother to write down her narrative of the family odyssey. The manuscript of Sarah Eleanor Royce presented in this volume is her answer to her son's request.

It must be thought of as a private document. In it Mrs. Royce expresses her thought without reserve. I suspect also that with hurrying pen she set down the record of the past which her memory retained. She seldom paused even to paragraph her work, thinking, no doubt, that her son would have little need for the refinements of style. The first part of her writing is a narrative of the gold rush as plain as the great majority of the Americans who made it. The latter sections suggest, with equal simplicity, what it meant to rear a brood in California in the riotous years which followed the great stampede. The western adventure which she describes was for Sarah Royce a fiery ordeal refining and tempering her character. With a frankness befitting the circle about the family fireside she presented to Josiah Royce a record of the attitudes and emotions of a sensitive and intelligent woman caught in a swirl of strange circumstance. Her tone suggests that the bond of sympathy was strong between her and her son. Royce dedicated his *California* to his mother.

The Royce manuscript loses much of its meaning, I think, unless it is read, as it was written, with Josiah Royce in mind. Even before he published his *California* in 1886 Royce was already one of a small group of pioneers who were blazing new trails for American thought. He lived in a period when industrialism was rapidly bringing a machine civilization to a bewildered people. Mark Twain, convinced that materialism was dominant in American life, referred to the times as the "Gilded Age." Josiah Royce was profoundly interested in the problems of life about him. The subtitle, "A Study of American Character," which he gave his *California,* suggests the direction of his thinking. Royce did not fail to see the materialism of the factories and the cities which were the offspring of industrialism. But he refused to surrender to pessimism. He possessed an almost Aristotelian mind and was a recognized master of logic. Before the end of the century Royce challenged the materialism of his age with a significant and original philosophy of idealism. His system commanded attention. His trowel helped to lay the foundations of twentieth-century thought.

To such a son, already embarked upon a career of intellectual pioneering, Mrs. Royce presented her intimate narrative of her own greatest years. The mood of her account seems to me more important than its details. It is the mood of the home from which Josiah Royce came. Such a fact alone gives the manuscript a niche in American intellectual history. But the writing has a larger significance. It reflects almost perfectly some important phases of mid-nineteenth-century American thinking.

The gold rush in which Mrs. Royce participated was, in a sense, a manifestation of that romantic spirit which stirred America in the early national period, the same spirit which in other realms expressed itself in the transcendentalism of Emerson and in the architecture of the Greek Revival. For many Americans the migration to California was a wistful search for a Never Never Land. It was such for Sarah Royce and her young husband trekking westward through hot summer days. Out of California gold they were spinning dreams of high endeavor. But this same gold rush was also a peculiarly striking expression of the materialism of pre-industrial America. The mad race for the yellow metal of California creek bottoms was only somewhat more dignified than the scramble of street arabs for pennies flung to the pavement. Mrs. Royce etches in a few strong lines the sordidness of the mining camps into which the streams of gold seekers debouched.

Equally vivid is Mrs. Royce's unplanned portrayal of the religion of the common people of America. She describes for the most part her own religious faith, a faith shared by thousands of her contemporaries. It might well be called Nineteenth-Century Puritanism. The old fear of Hell was fading and the devils of the seventeenth-century Puritans were almost forgotten. Mrs. Royce worshiped a deity whose relation to the poor affairs of men was governed by love. Had she remained in the East, it is possible that she might have gone through life merely a devout woman practicing the popular religion of her day. But the trip across the continent and life in early California strengthened the fiber of her faith. She ceased to be typical and came to portray Nineteenth-Century Puritanism at its best. On the plains east of the mountains she discovered the full meaning of loneliness. In the Carson desert she and her party escaped destruction by the narrowest margin. On those terrifying sands Sarah Royce worshiped God in a burning sage bush. She spoke to Him, and a strange, illogical peace was the answer to her prayer. She became a mystic and, from that hour, mysticism was one of the two foundation stones of her life.

The other rock upon which she built her career was the moral code which contained her formula for the good life. Unlike her son, she cared little for ethical theorizing. Her dominant interest was living. Her code was largely summed up in loyalty to her faith and to her family. The Royces unfortunately did not achieve sudden wealth. They paid dearly for their material gains. For many years they gave up the refinements of an established civilization and the repose of old communities. Friends of congenial mind and character were few. More than once home meant for Mrs. Royce a portable canvas house set up on the edge of unsightly diggings. Yet the narrative of Mrs. Royce is an account of a fundamentally happy experience. She found El Dorado in California but gold had little to do with its pavements or palaces. Sarah Royce discovered the good life in loyalty and mysticism.

One of the most important aspects of the Royce manuscript lies in the fact that it was written more than thirty years after most of its episodes had transpired. In the reconstruction of the journey across the continent Mrs. Royce was aided by her "Pilgrimage Diary" in which she had jotted notes by the way in 1849. The importance for her of her mystical experiences on the westward trek is made clear by the fact that, in later life, she emphasized them in her narrative to her son. As I read her story, I cannot, at times, escape the feeling that she is not merely narrating but is arguing with her philosopher son.

The mother of Josiah Royce cannot have been ignorant of the intellectual battle developing, in her later years, about her faith. From the middle of the nineteenth century Protestant orthodoxy, typified in the religion of Sarah Royce, was engaged in a fight for existence. Ranged behind breastworks of argument which had been centuries in building, the clergy of Nineteenth-Century Puritanism were stubbornly holding their ground against an effective fire from the geologists who were deciphering in the book of the rocks a narrative of earth history which had little resemblance to the biblical account. After 1859 the defenders faced an assault by a new army under a strange banner which bore the name of Darwin. Young Royce sailed for Germany to study philosophy with the dissonance of this battle in his ears. In the land of Hegel he discovered that historians were examining the scriptures in the same scientific spirit that they used in handling other documents and, by so doing, were organizing a flank attack upon the fieldworks of the old orthodoxy. By the time Royce's education was completed, the main positions of the Puritans had been carried. The Bible could no longer be considered in the old literal sense the inspired word of Deity. The theology which rested on a magic book was in ruins—the uncouth ruins of a battle-ravaged village after the guns have moved on and before vines have begun to grow over the ragged masonry.

Josiah Royce expressed the temper of the new intellectual age. "For us, the modern world is full of suggestions of doubt regarding the articles of the traditional creeds. The moral problems of our time, full of new complexities, confuse us with regard to what ought to be done. Our spiritual life is too complex to be any longer easily unified, or to be unified in ways useful for earlier generations. . . . Our sciences are too complicated to make it easy for us to conceive the world either as a unity or as spiritual." To a son whose philosophy was starting from such premises Sarah Royce reasserted in her narrative her loyalty to the old religion. In the private document which she wrote for him she included not only a narrative of events but, I believe, a confession of faith—a faith founded not upon a magic book but upon mystical experience. Not without significance are her closing words: "God . . . through all the devious paths of life ever guides safely those who trust and obey Him." In the writing of Mrs. Royce we hear a voice from old America speaking to a new age.

Josiah Royce was impressed but unconvinced by the argument from mysticism. He was even less convinced by the mechanistic concept of the universe set forth by the nineteenth-century physicists. Rejecting the materialism of his day he made significant contributions to modern idealism. "Every idealist," he remarked, "believes himself to have rational grounds for the faith that somewhere, and in some world, and at some time, the ideal will triumph, so that a survey, a divine synopsis of all time, somehow reveals the lesson of all sorrow, the meaning of all tragedy, the triumph of the spirit." Possessed of an amazing knowledge comprehending many disciplines and using logic for his tool Royce forged his philosophy of loyalty, his most important work.

This present book, in which his mother speaks, is no place for an elaborate discussion of the meaning and significance of the Royce philosophical system. A few sentences of his will bring us close to his basic ethical position. "If I am right," said Royce near the end of his life, "all the loyal are grasping in their own ways, and according to their own lights, some form and degree of religious truth. They have won religious insight; for they view something, at least, of the genuine spiritual world in its real unity, and they devote themselves to that unity, to its enlargement and its enrichment. And there they approach more and more to the comprehension of that true spiritual life whereof, as I suppose, the real world essentially consists. . . . In brief: Be loyal; grow in loyalty. Therein lies the source of a religious insight free from superstition. Therein . . . lies the solution of the problems of the philosophy of life." Therein, also, lay the secret of the life of Sarah Eleanor Royce. Her career was an almost perfect expression of Josiah Royce's philosophy of loyalty.

A FRONTIER LADY

That the life of his mother influenced the philosopher's thought there can be little doubt, but her importance for him is quite impossible to measure. I have tried to suggest in a fragmentary way the relation between the two by placing before each of the chapters, into which I have divided the narrative, a comment by Royce upon the type of life experience which is most conspicuously illustrated in the section.

RALPH HENRY GABRIEL.

New Haven, Connecticut,
  June, 1932.

Contents

CHAPTER I
Plains

I . . . have before me a manuscript, prepared by my mother for my use, wherein . . . she has narrated from her diary of that time, the story of the long land journey [to California]. . . . To strongly religious minds the psychological effect of this solitary struggle with the deserts was almost magical. One seemed alone with God in the waste, and felt but the thinnest veil separating a divine presence from the souls that often seemed to have no conceivable human resource left. This experience often expresses itself in language at once very homely and very mystical. God's presence, it declares, was no longer a matter of faith, but of direct sight. Who else was there but God in the desert to be seen? One was going on a pilgrimage whose every suggestion was of the familiar sacred stories. One sought a romantic and far-off golden land of promise, and one was in the wilderness of this world, often guided only by signs from heaven,—by the stars and by the sunset. The clear blue was almost perpetually overhead; the pure mountain winds were about one; and again even in the hot and parched deserts, a mysterious power provided the few precious springs and streams of water. Amid the jagged, broken, and barren hills, amid the desolation of the lonely plains, amid the half-unknown but always horrible dangers of the way, one met experiences of precisely the sort that elsewhere we always find producing the most enthusiastic forms of religious mysticism.

JOSIAH ROYCE, *California.*

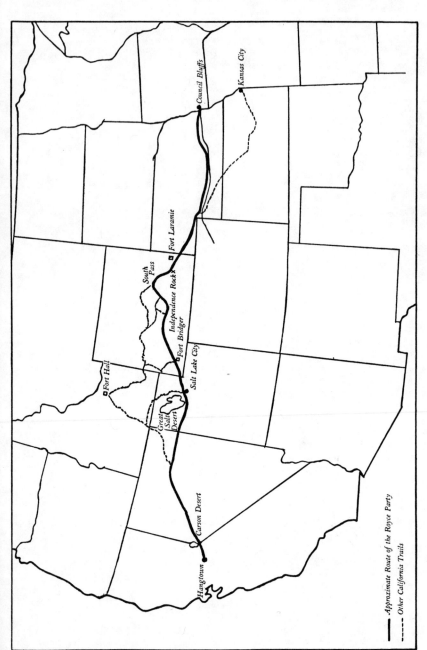

THE CALIFORNIA TRAILS IN 1849

Based on detailed maps by Archer B. Hulbert in *Transcontinental Trails*, Vol. IV

Plains

O N the last day of April, 1849 we began our journey to California. Our out-fit consisted of a covered wagon, well loaded with provisions, and such preparations for sleeping, cooking etc., as we had been able to furnish, guided only by the light of Fremont's *Travels*, and the suggestions, often conflicting, of the many who, like ourselves, utter strangers to camping life, were setting out for the "Golden Gate." Our wagon was drawn by three yoke of oxen and one yoke of cows, the latter being used in the team only part of the time. Their milk was of course to be a valuable part of our subsistence.

Nearly a year before we had bidden farewell to all our friends in the East, and we had been living for several months in a pleasant village in Iowa, about twenty miles from the Mississippi. So we had nearly the whole state of Iowa to cross, as merely introductory to the journey proper to California. Council Bluffs was the point for which we were to aim first, and that was to be the place of starting upon the grand pilgrimage.

The morning of that 30th of April was not very bright; but neither was it very gloomy. Rain might come within an hour, but then the sun might come out, —I would not consent to delay our departure for fear of the weather. Had I not made up my mind to encounter many storms? If we were going, let us go, and meet what we were to meet, bravely. So I seated myself in the wagon, my little two-year old Mary was placed

beside me, my husband and the other man of our little
company started the team, and we were on our way.
The day turned out by no means unpleasant. Our first
noon lunch was eaten by the whole party, seated in the
front part of the wagon, while the cattle, detached from
the wagon but not unyoked, grazed near by. After a
short rest we again moved on. The afternoon wore
quietly away, the weather being rather brighter and
warmer than in the morning,—and now night was coming on. No house was within sight.

Why did I look for one? I knew we were to camp; but
surely there would be a few trees or a sheltering hill-
side against which to place our wagon. No, only the
level prairie stretched on each side of the way. Nothing
indicated a place for us,—a cozy nook, in which for the
night we might be guarded, at least by banks and
boughs. I had for months anticipated this hour, yet, not
till it came, did I realize the blank dreariness of seeing
night come on without house or home to shelter us and
our baby-girl. And this was to be the same for many
weeks, perhaps months. It was a chilling prospect, and
there was a terrible shrinking from it in my heart; but
I kept it all to myself and we were soon busy making
things as comfortable as we could for the night. Our
wagon was large, we were provided with straw and
plenty of bed clothes; and soon a very tolerable resting
place was ready for us. Our little Mary had been happy
as a lark all day, and now sank to sleep in her straw
and blanket bed, as serenely as though she were in a
palace, on a downy pillow. At first the oppressive sense
of homelessness, and an instinct of watchfulness, kept
me awake. Perhaps it was not to be wondered at in one
whose life had so far, been spent in city or town, sur-

rounded by the accompaniments of civilization and who was now, for the first time in her life "camping out." However, quiet sleep came at last, and in the morning, there was a mildly exultant feeling which comes from having kept silent through a cowardly fit, and finding the fit gone off.

But the oxen and cows were found to be "gone off" too, and my first entry in my "Pilgrim's Diary" was made at very unwelcome leisure, "staying by the stuff" with my little one, while the men were recovering the animals. It was late in the forenoon when they were brought and yoked up, and our second days journey was begun. It soon became plain that the hard facts of this pilgrimage would require patience, energy, and courage fully equal to what I had anticipated when I had tried to stretch my imagination to the utmost. These facts came first in such mean, vexing forms. Deep mud-holes in which the wagon would stick fast, or, still worse, sloughs,—called by the western people "sloos," —covered with turf that appeared perfectly sound, but which would break when the full weight came upon it, and let the wheels in nearly to the hubs; closing round the spokes so tightly that digging, alone, would free them. In these cases, the whole, or nearly the whole, of the contents of the wagon had to be unloaded, often in very miry places sometimes in the rain, while the men had to "put shoulder to the wheels" and lift them out by main force. Several times while we were all busy, in such a scene the cattle wandered off, into a wood or over a hill, and hours would be lost in getting them to-gether. Oftener they were lost in the morning,—for they must be turned out to graze during the night, and then the best traveling part of the day would be gone, before we could move on. This happened on our fourth day out.

Looking into my old diary, which I kept in those days, though in a very broken, desultory manner, I find the following entry, for May 3rd, 1849. "The sloughs were very bad, stopping us repeatedly during the day; and just at dusk we found ourselves fast, in a most dreary swamp." We had encountered in the middle of the afternoon a tremendous blow and rain while out on the open prairie,—the night looked threatening, and before morning we were visited by a heavy thunder storm. The next day, Friday, was so inclement as to prevent traveling. I cooked as well as I could by a log fire in a strong north-east blow. My little Mary, to my great surprise, was cheerful and happy, playing in the wagon, with various simple things I provided for her, singing and laughing most of the time.

Saturday morning, though the weather still continued cloudy, we attempted to proceed, but the rain had softened the ground so much that we found ourselves "*stuck*" almost every half mile. After a hard day's work we succeeded in reaching the little town of Tipton, only three miles from where we started in the morning. Here we spent our first Sabbath out; the clouds still threatening and the rain falling every few minutes. At this point we met with three other wagons, and three days after, at Cedar River, with several others, all bound for California. There was certainly satisfaction in having company, for we could, by uniting teams help each other over hard places, saving much time. But the weather still continued unfavorable, and I find recorded for Friday, May 11th, which was the day after crossing the Cedar River, that "we had a hard day's drive through a drenching rain, arriving at Iowa City toward night." Here we spent our second Sunday, and on Monday morning crossed the Iowa River which I see I noted as "A pretty stream, reminding me of my own, old Genesee; especially when I saw one, solitary steamboat lying at the landing some distance from the City."

Storms, bad roads and swollen streams, continued to impede our way nearly every day till we reached Council Bluffs. Referring again to my journal, I find on the 20th of May we "were visited by a thunder storm," and, on the 21st, "Were overtaken, during the afternoon by two tremendous storms of thunder, lightning and wind. Encamped, just as the last one burst upon us, on the lee side of a beautiful grove; and, at the close of the storm, as the clouds broke, the most brilliant and perfect rain-bow I ever saw completely arched the lovely scene."

"May 22. Reached Indian Creek which was so swollen by the late rains as to be impassable. Had to remain there until the men built a bridge; which took them till the next day at noon; and after crossing the stream, our way for some distance lay through flat, bottomland, where in several places the water stood two feet deep."

When we reached Fort Des Moines we fell in with several more little companies from different points, nearly all of whom gave discouraging reports of their own progress, and of the news they were receiving, at this point, in various ways, from others who were on the way to California. From Council Bluffs, and other crossing places on the Missouri River, came word that cholera was raging among the emigrants; with various

other depressing stories about difficulties in obtaining
proper supplies of wholesome provisions, such as could
be carried on so long a journey. To this was added the
assertion that such an immense number had already left
the Missouri, and were far on their way, that the grass
was all eaten up, and no more animals could live on the
great plains.

All this we heard, and all this we talked over, but
still we went on, and at the end of one month and four
days after beginning our travels, we reached Council
Bluffs. Here we found a city of wagons, some of which
had been there many days waiting their turn to cross
the great river. But we were consoled by being assured
that the ferry men were working as fast as possible, and
that probably in a week or so, all now camped ready
for crossing, would be over the Missouri. Notwithstanding the crowd of people, most of them strangers to each
other, thrown together in such new and inconvenient
circumstances, with much to try patience—and all
standing necessarily more or less in the position of
rivals for the local conveniences which campers so soon
learn to look for and prize—still the utmost quiet and
good humor . . . prevailed. The great majority of the
crowd were men, generally working men of ordinary intelligence, farmers and mechanics—accustomed to the
comforts and amenities of domestic life, and, most of
them evidently intending to carry more or less of these
agreeable things with them 'across the plains.' Occasionally these men were accompanied by wife and children, and their wagons were easily distinguished by the
greater number of conveniences, and house-hold articles
they carried, which here, in this time of prolonged
camping, were often, many of them, disposed about the

outside of the wagon, in a home-like way. And, where
bushes, trees or logs formed partial enclosures, a
kitchen or sitting room quite easily suggested itself to a
feminine heart, yearning for home. The few women who
caught glimpses of each other, or, in some cases, were
thrown nearer together in this motley gathering were in
general very kind to each other, and to each other's
children. But, waiting as they were for the very first
chance to cross the Missouri, and expecting after that
to travel in different companies, there was no motive for
any particular mutual interest.

After patiently waiting some days for our turn to
cross the river, it came at last, and on Friday the 8th
of June we ventured ourselves and our little all, on
board a very uncertain looking ferryboat and were
slowly conveyed across the turbid and unfriendly-look-
ing Missouri. The cattle were "swum" across the
stream; the men driving them in and frightening them
off from the shore in various ways, until a few of the
leaders reached the flats on the opposite side. As soon as
they were seen to come out of the water there, the others
easily followed. A few of the many thus crossed were
driven by the strong current beyond the flats and lost,
but most of them crossed safely. From the place where
we landed the ascent up the bluff was steep and dusty.
Arriving at the top we were on an almost level plain,
with only here and there a tree or two, though there was
a body of timber a mile or two to the southwest. Not
very far from the river we began to see the few scatter-
ing buildings of Trader's Point, the Indian Agency for
this part of Nebraska Territory.

So few . . . were the houses that I scarcely remember any thing but a blacksmith's shop and, not far from

it, a pretty good sized log house. Yet, on that spot
Omaha City soon after grew to fair proportions, and
has now for many years flourished. A slight accident
had broken something about the wagon, and we stopped
at the blacksmith-shop to have it repaired. The other
wagons passed on to the place of encampment for the
night which was to be in the edge of the before mentioned timber. Just as the blacksmith began work on
our wagon, the gentlemanly Indian Agent, whom we had
seen at Council Bluffs, came to us and kindly insisted
upon my going, with my little girl to his home, which
proved to be the good-sized log house I had noticed, and
resting there till my husband was ready to proceed. I
gratefully accepted, and his hospitality did not cease
until we had all three partaken of a bountiful supper
prepared by his kind-hearted old negro cook, and had
enjoyed a good rest and social chat beside his ample
fire place. He then helped us into our wagon, directed
us to our camp grounds, two miles distant, expressed
his good wishes for our long journey, and bade us good
night. That was my farewell to the fag-end of civilization on the Atlantic side of the continent. I saw no
house from that time till we passed within view of the
few dwellings at Fort Laramie; and did not again eat
a meal in a house, until urged to do so once only by a
hospitable Mormon woman, beside whose garden fence
we had permission to locate our wagon, during our stay
in Salt Lake City.

From our first arrival at Council Bluffs we had been
annoyed by begging and pilfering Indians, male and
female. To attempt to satisfy them was out of the question, for the most trifling thing bestowed on one, would
bring a dozen more. So our only defence was to keep

them decidedly and quietly at a distance. Few of them could understand our words and we had to act with most emphatic dignity to keep them at all in their proper place. On the western side of the Missouri they became more numerous, swarming about us at every pause in our way from the crossing of the ferry till night closed in, but then they disappeared; and the agent assured us that they were gone, not "to bed," but to their sleep among the bushes and sand hills; and that they would not dare to molest us so near the Agency; so, we might go, without fear, to camp. His words proved true, and we arrived safely at our place of stopping for the first night in an Indian country.

The next day was spent mostly by the men in organizing a regular company, with captain, and subordinate officers whose duties and prerogatives were set forth in rules and by-laws then and there adopted. The few women in the company were busy meantime in cooking, washing, mending up clothes, etc. Notwithstanding the disheartening reports circulated among us for the past two weeks at different points in our way, hopefulness and unflinching resolution upon the whole prevailed. Some few there were, no doubt, who would have turned back, but they were involved either in family or business relations with others more resolute—or more rash—and, seeing the uselessness of resistance, they took up their part of the daily toil, in most cases, without complaining.

A number in the company tried to incorporate in the by-laws, a rule that every Sunday should be a day of rest; but they only succeeded in gaining a general assent to camping on Sundays when the necessities and dangers of the way did not demand uninterrupted trav-

eling. The majority insisted that the lateness of the
season,—we being nearly the last emigrants to cross the
Missouri,—and the importance of keeping near to
larger companies just ahead, made it imperative that
we should set out the very next morning; although it
was Sunday. Accordingly on the 10th of June we left
our first camp ground west of the Missouri, and
launched forth upon a journey in which, we all knew,
from that hour there was not the least chance of turning back.

The morning was bright and the scene animating. We
were up early, breakfast was dispatched, and then came
the bustle of packing our wagons, which was done by
one man belonging to each wagon, while the other one,
or two yoked the cattle. In the few cases where there
were women they were, without exception, seen doing
their full share of the work. When all was ready the Captain gave the word of command, "Roll out!" and wagon
after wagon fell into line in the order which had been
assigned them. For an hour or two we moved on with as
lively a pace as oxen could well keep up. The sun shone
brightly, and all looked hopeful. We were approaching
rolling hills between which, we could see, our road lay.

[*The party was taking what was called the Mormon
Trail, which ran on the north side of the Platte River
from Council Bluffs to Fort Laramie. It was now in the
heart of the country where the Plains Indians followed
and lived upon the bison herds. Roving bands of hunt-
ers, Pawnees, Sioux, Cheyennes, Poncas, mounted on
lean, half-broken ponies, rode back and forth across the
grasslands through which ran the emigrant trail. Villages as mobile as an army, moved swiftly, seeking food
and plunder. The redskins had long known the white*

*man as a trader who scattered palisaded forts through
their country. Of late years they had become familiar
with the emigrant trains plodding westward. The
painted warriors respected the trader because he knew
their ways and met them with a boldness and a cunning
equal to their own. But the emigrants from eastern
farms and cities were men of different quality. Feath-
ered headdresses filled them with consternation. They
could often be bullied by insolent demands. In the summer of 1849 the tribes of the plains, bewildered, appre-
hensive, resentful, greedy, watched an unprecedented
flood of white interlopers pass through their hunting
grounds.]*

Suddenly, numerous dark moving objects appeared
upon the hills in the distance, on both sides of the road.
What could they be? Had some of the large companies
ahead camped, and turned out their cattle? Or, could
it be, that we were about to have our first sight of a
herd of buffalo? As we drew nearer they proved to be
Indians, by hundreds; and soon they had ranged themselves along on each side of the way. A group of them
came forward, and at the Captain's command our company halted, while he with several others went to meet
the Indians and hold a parley. It turned out that they
had gathered to demand the payment of a certain sum
per head for every emigrant passing through this part
of the country, which they claimed as their own. The
men of our company after consultation, resolved that
the demand was unreasonable! that the country we were
traveling over belonged to the United States, and that
these red men had no right to stop us. The Indians were
then plainly informed that the company meant to proceed at once without paying a dollar. That if unmo-

lested, they would not harm anything; but if the Indians attempted to stop them, they would open fire with all their rifles and revolvers. At the Captain's word of command all the men of the company then armed themselves with every weapon to be found in their wagons. Revolvers, knives, hatchets, glittered in their belts; rifles and guns bristled on their shoulders. The drivers raised aloft their long whips, the rousing words "Go 'long Buck"—"Bright!"—"Dan!" were given all along the line, and we were at once moving between long but not very compact rows of half naked redskins; many of them well armed; others carrying but indifferent weapons; while all wore in their faces the expression of sullen disappointment, mingled with a half-defiant scowl, that suggested the thought of future night attacks, when darkness and thickets should give them greater advantage. For the present, however, they had evidently made up their minds to let us pass, and we soon lost sight of them.

But another enemy, unseen, and without one audible word of demand or threat, was in that very hour advancing upon us, and made our wagon his first point of attack. The oldest of the men who had joined company with my husband, complained of intense pain and sickness, and was soon obliged to lie down in the wagon, which, being large, gave room for quite a comfortable bed behind the seat where Mary and I sat. Soon, terrible spasms convulsed him; the Captain was called, examined the case, and ordered a halt. Medicine was administered which afforded some relief. About this time a horseman or two appeared, with the intelligence that some companies in advance of us were camped at the ford of the Elkhorn River, not more than two miles distant, and that there was a physician among them. We therefore made the sick man as comfortable as we could, and went on. Arrived at the encampment the Doctor pronounced the disease Asiatic Cholera. Everything was done that could be under the circumstances, but nothing availed, and in two or three hours the poor old man expired.

The most prompt and energetic sympathy was shown by our fellow travelers. The fact was at once recognized that close contact with the disease for several hours, had exposed us to contagion, and had also made necessary the disinfecting of our wagon and all it contained. There were in the encampment those who had tents as well as wagons, and soon a comfortable tent, with a cot bed and other conveniences, was placed at our disposal till our things could be disinfected. That Sunday night was one never to be forgotten by me. I positively refused to lie down, because there was room and covering for only one besides Mary—my husband had been on guard the night before, and on most exhausting duty all day; so I insisted upon his resting, while I sat by my little one, leaning my head on her pillow, and tried to sleep.

But a storm began in the evening. The wind moaned fitfully, and rain fell constantly. I could not sleep. I rose and walked softly to the tent door, put the curtains aside and looked out. The body of the dead man lay stretched upon a rudely constructed bier beside our wagon a few rods off, the sheet that was stretched over it flapped in the wind with a sound that suggested the idea of some vindictive creature struggling restlessly in bonds; while its white flutterings, dimly seen, confirmed the ghastly fancy. Not many yards beyond, a party of Indians—who had, for a day or two, been playing the part of friendly hangers-on to one of the large companies—had raised a rude skin tent, and built a fire, round which they were seated on the ground,—looking unearthly in its flickering light, and chanting, hour after hour, a wild melancholy chant, varied by occasional high, shrill notes as of distressful appeal. The minor key ran through it all. I knew it was a death dirge.

Morning came at last. In the early dawn the body of the old man was laid in the grave that had been dug in a hill-side nearby. Then came the work of cleansing the wagon, washing bed clothes and thoroughly sunning and airing everything; for the storm was over and the sun shone very warmly. Before we had half done this work, the crossing of the Elkhorn was begun by the other companies. The wagons and people crossed on rafts and the cattle were "swum." By one or two o'clock P.M. we were all across and we finished our drying and airing on the west side. Soon after leaving the Elkhorn we struck the Platte River and now felt ourselves fairly launched out "on the plains."

The next Wednesday morning, June 13th, before dawn we were visited by one of the most terrible storms I ever recollect witnessing. Thunder, lightning and wind seemed combined to tear our frail tenements to pieces; but the same Almighty Power that sent the tempest, tempered it to us defenseless ones; and though the rain drove into our wagons, our food and clothing were not seriously injured. The next morning, just three days from the time old Mr. R—— had been buried, the first news that met our ears was, that two more of our company were ill with the same fatal disease. Before the first watch of that night was set, one of them was laid in his lonely grave. I here quote again from my diary, which I "wrote up" a few days after these events.

"Now indeed a heavy gloom hung round us. The destroyer seemed let loose upon our camp. Who would go next? What if my husband should be taken and leave us alone in the wilderness? What if I should be taken and leave my little Mary motherless? Or, still more distracting thought—what if we both should be laid low, and she be left a destitute orphan, among strangers, in a land of savages? Such thoughts would rush into my mind, and for some hours these gloomy forebodings heavily oppressed me; but I poured out my heart to God in prayer, and He gave me comfort and rest. I felt a full assurance that He would not afflict us beyond our strength to bear. I committed my precious child into His hands entirely, claiming for her His promises, and His guardianship. I said from my heart 'Thy will be done.' Then peace took possession of my soul, and spite of threatening ills, I felt strong for duty and endurance."

The second of the two sick men soon began to show favorable symptoms and in a few days recovered. From that time we had no more cases of cholera among our fellow travelers; though we passed a number of graves of its victims, and heard of deaths in other companies who camped not far from us.

On Saturday evening June 16th we arrived at the crossing of the Loup Fork of the Platte River. Here we found two companies, who had been camped there some days waiting for the waters to go down so that they could find a fording place. The bed of the Loup is, for miles, formed of quick-sand, so that where teams crossed in safety one day there might be deep holes the next. Especially after the waters had been swollen by heavy rains as had lately been the case, it was impossible to be sure of a fording place without the most careful exploration, which of course involved considerable danger. A man had been drowned only a short time before our arrival, by venturing too hastily forward, when nearly across. He had found the water so shallow thus far, that he became too sanguine, and stepped suddenly into a deep channel, where the rushing water and sand soon swallowed him up.

On the third day it was announced that the water had sufficiently subsided for us to attempt the passage; though there was still rather an ugly current near the farther shore. On our side there was shallow water for some rods through which our ordinary teams could pull a lightly-loaded wagon. Then there was an island of sand; and beyond that, the current was so deep and strong that teams would have to be doubled, and long ropes used. Moreover the greatest dispatch was necessary; for the sands shifted so constantly that the bottom changed more or less every hour. As the quickest way of working, our own teams were to take to the island two or three wagons at a time, then, fastening all the cattle to one wagon, with several men to drive, they were to rush that one rapidly across the deeper stream, and return for another. As fast as one standing-place on the island was vacated another wagon was driven over the shallow water to be ready for its turn; and thus one fresh team was used to each wagon at the hardest point. It was a little exciting for us women to take our seats, with our children beside us, and be drawn upon those treacherous sands we had heard so much of for two or three days; and it became startling when we felt the wagon trembling under us, as in a lively earthquake. The vibrations did not cease while we stood on the island, the wheels perpetually settling with short jerks into the sand: had we been obliged to stay there long we should have sunk to the hubs. But the men and faithful cattle worked nobly, and in due time we were west of the treacherous Loup Fork.

A few days after this we had a new and unexpected experience in the way of a stampede of cattle. On camping for the night each company of wagons always formed a corral by placing the wagons one before the other in such a position as to make a large circle. The tongue of each wagon dropped its end to the ground, as the cattle were loosed from it, and the wagon in front was backed up so close as to leave barely room for a person to step in and out. A space, large enough to form a gateway, was left between the back of the first wagon and the front of the last, and into this gateway the cattle were driven at night, after they had well pastured; and the gateway was closed by ox-chains, securely fastened to the wheels of the two terminating wagons. Then a guard of two or three men, was set, who patrolled on the outside of the corral, and were changed after midnight. On the night of the 19th of June our wagon was one of the terminating ones with its back to the gateway. On Wednesday morning June 20th I was awakened between three and four o'clock, by the sound of rain upon the wagon-top. It was quite a moderate shower, and I lay thinking, in a calm mood, when a flash of lightning came, followed in a moment by a strange, rushing sound, which quickly became loud as thunder. The wagon began to shake violently, then to move as if pushed sideways by a great force, then it was lifted and thrown violently over on its side; there was a crash of breaking wheels and chains, the rapid tramp of cattle became distinct for a minute, and then was lost in the distance.

When we and our neighbors on the other side of the gateway, had picked ourselves up, and out, and found that none of us were much hurt, we began to try to account for the catastrophe, and examine its extent. The cattle must have been frightened by the flash of lightning. Those near the entrance of the corral instinctively tried to escape, others near, pressed upon them, the panic grew, till, in their frantic struggles, they overturned the two chained wagons. At that moment the chains must have broken and cleared the passage-way, or they would have trampled us to death. There were some unimportant injuries done to both the wagons and to some of their contents; but the grand calamity was the breaking of three wheels; one of ours, and two of the other. We had, a day or two before, entered upon a stage of the journey marked in our guide-books as being destitute of timber for nearly two hundred miles, with the exception of one, solitary tree—about midway of the distance—marked down as "The Lone Tree." Just as we had found out the worst of our breakage, the Captain of the company came near, and, after gazing a moment in speechless consternation, exclaimed, "Three wheels broke all to smash, and fifty miles from timber!" It was true, and the fact was a hard one, yet, strange elasticity of mind, we laughed heartily at the grotesque speech.

But now, what was to be done? In the first place, the cattle had "stampeded," and were all gone. How, and when could they be got back? Often in such cases they ran themselves to death. But even while we thus questioned, we were told that at the first alarm, some of the men had mounted the few horses owned in the company, and were last seen gaining upon the swiftest fugitives; while others, on foot, had already succeeded in turning back some of the more gentle ones. But those broken wheels—how could they be repaired in this desert? It soon turned out that there was a blacksmith in the company, with some tools, and a few odd pieces of hard wood; there were also two families who had brought with them wide, hard-wood boards, two or three feet long, which they used for tables while camping. These were freely contributed to the necessities of the occasion; and, as some of the spokes of the broken wheels were still whole, as well as parts of the rims, it was soon decided that enough material for repairs was at hand, though we *were* 'fifty miles from timber.' In a few hours the lost cattle were all recovered, and had plenty of time to rest and feed while the wagons were mended, which took all the remainder of that day, and the whole of the next.

From this time for several days we went on, with nothing special to mark our progress, except passing the "Lone Tree," which I made into an event to myself, by straining my eyes to get the first glimpse of it, watching its change from the first dim uncertainty, till it stood distinct in the distance, awaiting our approach; then mentally holding converse with it, as I drew near; questioning how it felt, standing there all alone, not one of its kindred within sight? How long it had thus stood? What strange cause had led to its life of isolation? Had the thousands of human beings who had passed it before us this season, cheered its old lone heart as their voices vibrated among its branches? Had any of them been cheered by observing its greenness, or resting in its shade? It was not a large tree but its branches, covered with foliage, formed a well rounded canopy for two or three. To me it was an impressive way-mark, which I passed with lingering steps, as I breathed silent thanksgivings for the "Hitherto" in which "the Lord had led us." As long as it remained in sight I cast frequent backward looks; feeling almost as though we were forsaking a living creature to the solitude of the desert.

July 1st at noon, we were camping near a large company whom we had overtaken when one or two horsemen came from the rear, with the information that the company to which they belonged, and which was very small, had become alarmed at the motions of some Indians who had made their appearance an hour or two before, and seemed preparing to attack them. The white men had, from a rising ground seen the dust of our company ahead, and had sent to ask aid. Very promptly, thirty or forty men from our company and the one near us, volunteered to answer the call, armed themselves and left us; while, those remaining, turned all the wagons into one corral and set guard. In two or three hours the others returned, with the report that the Indians had left, as soon as they saw superior numbers.

On the morning of July 4th we passed some remarkable rocks called Ancient Bluff Ruins [probably Court House Rock] and came within sight of Chimney Rock, an immense natural tower visible for many miles, before, and after, we passed it. In the afternoon we halted to celebrate the day. In one tent, a few gathered for a dance; in another several of us old fashioned people enjoyed a cheerful "sing."

[*The Royce party were still in the valley of the Platte. Since the crossing at Loup Fork they had been following the well-known trail which clung to the southern bank of that river. The summer was advancing and they were far behind the van of the gold rush. For nearly a month the party had been traversing the bison country. The explanation of Mrs. Royce's failure to mention any sight of these animals is probably to be found in the fact that the earlier Forty-niners in hunting for meat drove the herds far from the trail.*]

We were now within about a hundred miles of Fort Laramie and, in a day or two, began to look out for Laramie Peak. We first descried it as a faint cloud on the horizon, but the next day it became more distinct, and soon, its snow-covered top formed a cheering contrast to the monotony that had marked our view for so long. On the evening of July 9th we camped within three miles of Fort Laramie. Here we remained, resting, and recruiting the cattle, until the afternoon of the 11th when we crossed the Platte River, passed the Fort, near sunset, amid a glorious thunder storm, and camped a mile and a half beyond. We now soon entered the Black Hills and the scenery became varied. July 15th we passed in the morning the northern foot of Laramie Peak, and saw a splendid thunder storm circling about its venerable brow.

At noon of the same day, we camped in a beautiful grove through which a clear mountain stream wound its way. It was a tempting place to tarry awhile, and it seems we did not hurry to break up our mid-day halt;

for I find in my diary a lengthened entry under that date, closing thus: "I have found a quiet spot at a little distance from the wagons, where I am seated on a stone, with book and pencil in hand, the babbling brook just at my feet, and close beside me, my little Mary who is picking up the colored pebbles and throwing them, with exclamations of delight into the sparkling waters."

But these pleasant surroundings were exchanged, in a day or two, for a region of great scarcity of feed, the hills being originally not very productive, and the great numbers of cattle preceding us this summer, having eaten all feed near the road. The 17th of July, toward evening, we camped at Deer Creek, a branch of the Platte. The ground was utterly destitute of vegetation, though there were plenty of trees to give us shade. The men of the company now divided into two bands. The elderly ones, and the two or three having families were detailed to stay with the wagons; keeping one or two horses with them while the others, taking with them the other horses, drove the cattle up the creek valley, searching for feed. They had to go fifteen miles up the stream before they found a sufficiency; but there they came into a very rich valley, in which the poor animals luxuriated and rested for two days, communication being kept up between the two divisions of our company by means of the horses.

Soon after resuming our journey we again crossed the Platte River to the north side. And now, once more, a terrific storm overtook us. Thunder, lightning, wind, hail and rain, poured their fury upon us. The terrified cattle were hastily detached from the wagons, and herded as near as possible to the lee side of the hill; but it was with the greatest difficulty they were kept from a stampede. This was on the 21st of July. A day or two afterward, we came upon the Sweetwater River, so named by Frémont and his men, on account of its water being so much better than any they had tasted for several days before. It was indeed a pretty stream, and we began to ascend it with renewed spirits, knowing that when we reached its head we should soon pass the summit of the Rocky Mountains.

July 26th we reached Independence Rock, where Frémont and his men spent the Fourth of July when they explored this route, and named the Rock accordingly. It is a bare mass of rock, without vegetation, rising directly from the flat, sandy land bordering the river, and detached entirely from any other elevation. Its general outline is round, though somewhat irregular; and at a distance one might fancy it an enormous elephant kneeling down. The least precipitous side was broken by irregular projections and narrow ledges, affording foothold for those willing to do some hard climbing. I had long before determined to ascend it, if I ever reached it, and found it not too rash an undertaking. Another woman of our company joined me. One or two of her boys climbed with us, and (just that she might have it to remember, and tell of) I took my little Mary. Of course I had to lift her from one projection to another most of the way; but we went leisurely, and her delight on reaching the top, our short rest there and the view we enjoyed, fully paid for the labor.

[*Independence Rock had, since Frémont's day, been the most famous landmark on the overland trail. It is a lone mass of granite somewhat more than fifteen hundred yards in circumference rising at its highest point one hundred ninety-three feet above the plain.*]

On Sunday the 29th of July we determined to remain in camp and rest till the next day. One family of our fellow travelers, Mr. B—— and his wife with their three little boys, did the same. We enjoyed a quiet rest, held a social meeting for prayer, reading and singing, and the next morning resumed our journey, much refreshed. From this time till we reached Salt Lake we had no earthly company or protection except that mutually afforded and enjoyed by two men, two women and four children, the oldest not more than eight, and the youngest not yet three. Twice we met with Indians, but they did not molest us. We passed the company we had been traveling with, kept in advance of them, notwithstanding Sunday rests, and arrived in Salt Lake valley the day before they did. But to return to our first week of lone traveling. For five days we kept on up the Sweetwater, and on Friday night encamped near its head. Not far from this, we made our nearest approach to the foot of Frémont's Peak, of which we had a grand view as we walked beside our wagon. Saturday the 4th of August we reached the South Pass of the Rocky Mountains.

Our Guide Book gave very elaborate directions by which we might be able to identify the highest point in our road, where we passed from the Atlantic to the Pacific Slope. Otherwise we could not have noticed it, so gradual had been the ascent, and so slightly varied was the surface for a mile or two on all sides. But I had looked forward for weeks to the step that should take me past that point. In the morning of that day I had taken my last look at the waters that flowed eastward, to mingle with the streams and wash the shores where childhood and early youth had been spent; where all I loved, save, O, so small a number, lived; and now I stood on the almost imperceptible elevation that, when passed, would separate me from all these, perhaps forever.)Through what toils and dangers we had come to reach that point; and, as I stood looking my farewell, a strong desire seized me to mark the spot in some way, and record at least one word of grateful acknowledgment. Yes, I would make a little heap of stones, and mark on one of them, or on a stick, the word "Ebenezer."

[*Ebenezer, stone of help, a place a few miles north of Jerusalem where Samuel set up a stone to commemorate a victory over the Philistines. "Then Samuel took a stone, and set it between Mizpeh and Shen, and called the name of it Ebenezer, saying, Hitherto hath the Lord helped us."*]

Nobody would notice or understand it; but my Heavenly Father would see the little monument in the mountain wilderness, and accept the humble thanks it recorded. So I turned to gather stones. But no stone could I find, not even pebbles enough to make a heap,— and no stick either, not a bush or a shrub or a tree within reach. So I stood still upon the spot till the two wagons and the little company had passed out of hearing; and when I left not a visible sign marked the place.

We were now for several days crossing the extreme northern end of the great Colorado Valley. Many of the springs were so strong with alkali as to be powerfully poisonous, and the grass in their vicinity was the same. One of our oxen died on the second day after entering this section, and we were obliged to yoke up the rest, and travel all night, so as to get to safer feed and water. On Saturday of that week we camped at night by Black Fork where we rested over Sunday. The next day reached Fort Bridger where was a rude log fort and one or two log huts. We got what information we could about the road and passed on.

[*The season was already late. At Fort Bridger the Royce party passed the last of the trails leading to Fort Hall. The Fort Hall route, so well known to the emigrants going to Oregon earlier in the decade, offered a safe course around the desert country which lay immediately west of Great Salt Lake. But this trail exacted many extra miles of traveling as the price of safety. The Royces could not risk the longer way for fear of being stopped by winter at the eastern end of the passes of the Sierras.*]

The next day August 14th we crossed the dividing ridge between the Colorado Valley and the Great Salt Lake Basin. Here, in the Wasatch Mountains, our road was by far the most precipitous and the scenery the wildest, we had yet seen. At the greatest elevation our altitude was seven thousand some hundred feet. Looking up to the high peak which towered above us on our left, we distinctly saw snow driving and eddying about in the strong wind. The clouds settled down nearer to us and we had a lively sprinkling of rain for a short time, but as we descended we were soon again in the hot sunshine; the dust, which had been excessive for two days, growing deeper and deeper, lighter and lighter, till it was like wading through a bed of fine ashes; so that when, at the entrance of Great Salt Lake Valley, we paused to take breath, and faced each other with mutual looks of wonder, we agreed that we did not know each other; and it was not till after a free use of the pure valley waters, aided in some instances by the hot mineral springs, that we recovered our identity.

It was near sunset on the 18th of August when we got our first view of the Great Salt Lake, with its back-ground of mountains; and in its foreground the well laid-out city, of snug dwellings and thrifty gardens. The suddenness with which we came upon the view was startling. From narrow mountain gorges and rough crooked turns, our road abruptly led us through an opening, almost like an immense doorway, unarched at the top. Here we were on a small plateau some hundreds of feet above the valley, with nothing to obstruct one's view for many miles. It is impossible to describe how, in the transparent atmosphere, everything was brought out with a distinctness that almost ignored distance. From here the road wound gradually down the mountain side to the plain and then into the City. As it was near sunset we camped on the second plateau, rested there through Sunday, and then moved into the City of Great Salt Lake.

At this point, company organizations were broken up, almost without exception, and every man proceeded to make such arrangements as seemed best to himself and those belonging to the same wagon. In many cases, even those owning teams and wagons together, sold out and parted goods, each taking his own way. Some few hurried on at once, but nearly all remained, a few days at least, to recruit. There was a general selling of tired out cattle; and buying of fresh.

CHAPTER II

Desert

The journey westward to California is . . . a dramatic series of incidents. From the wide plains of the states immediately west of the Mississippi one passes at first through richly fertile regions to the more and more arid prairies of the eastern slope of the Rocky Mountains. Then come either the steep ranges or the wide passes, and at last what used to be called the Great American Desert itself, that great interior basin of the rugged, saw-tooth ranges, where the weirdly dreary landscape at once terrifies the observer by its desolation, and inspires him by the grandeur of its loneliness, and by the mysterious peacefulness of the desert wherein, as one at first feels, nothing like the complex and restless life of our eastern civilization will ever be possible.

As one travels by the familiar central route still farther west, one reaches the valley of the Humboldt River, that kindly stream whose general westerly trend made the early overland migration possible. At the end of this portion of the route rises the vast wall of the Sierra Range, and the traveler's heart thrills with something of the strange feeling that the early immigrants described when, after their long toil, they reached the place where, just beyond this dark and deathlike wall, the land of heavenly promise was known to lie.

JOSIAH ROYCE, *The Pacific Coast*

Desert

SOON, notice was formally circulated among the emigrants that a certain man, whose name I forget, professing to be an experienced traveler, and explorer of the Great Basin, would lead a company to California by a route far south of the one followed by emigrants thus far. He would start from Salt Lake City a month or two later, and he strongly advised tired travelers to remain and rest themselves, and then join his party. We heard all this, and discussed it.

[The Royce party decided against waiting to go by the "new southern route" and prepared, in spite of the lateness of the season, to follow the usual trail from Great Salt Lake west via the Humboldt River and the Carson Desert to the Sierras.]

We also heard the warnings, and saw the solemnly shaken heads of the Mormon Prophets. They told us we would lose our cattle and perish on the desert; or, if we reached the Sierras, would be snowed in and perish there. We heard it, we coolly talked it over, and yet, so perverse were we, that on the 30th day of August, a solitary wagon, drawn by three yoke of oxen, and in charge of only two men, left Salt Lake City, bearing, as its passengers, one woman and one little child, and for freight only so much provisions as might last us till we could scale the great Sierras and reach their western foot.

[The Royces had by now become virtually the rear party of the overland Forty-niners. They chose the route which crossed the forbidding and dangerous Great Salt Desert immediately west of Great Salt Lake.

[33]

Thence they followed a westerly course across broken country to the Humboldt River.]

Our only guide from Salt Lake City consisted of two small sheets of note paper, sewed together, and bearing on the outside in writing the title "Best Guide to the Gold Mines, 816 miles, by Ira J. Willes, GSL City."

This little pamphlet was wholly in writing, there being at that time no printing press at Salt Lake. It was gotten up by a man who had been to California and back the preceding year. The directions, and the descriptions of camping places, together with the distances seemed pretty definite and satisfactory until they reached the lower part of the Mary's or Humboldt River; when poor camping and scarcity of water were mentioned with discouraging frequency. From the sink of the Humboldt, all seemed confusion. We were told by our writer, to look out for a new track which "was to be made last fall" and which *"might be better,"* and just here, for several stages, all seemed uncertainty. Indeed the man from whom we got the Guide Book told my husband he must be guided in this part of the way, by information which he must get from a returning Mormon Train, which we would meet before reaching the Humboldt.

The only man who now accompanied my husband was considerably advanced in years, and not in perfect health. He was extremely anxious to reach California, but had no means in the world save one solitary ox, a little clothing and sufficient food to sustain him till he reached El Dorado, if he could go straight through. He offered to put his ox into the team, to help drive and take care of the cattle and assist otherwise, so far as able, for the privilege of traveling in company and having his few things carried. Thus we set forth on the last, and by far the most perilous, stage of our great journey.

We had traveled but a few days, when, after camping one evening, we saw approaching, a couple of young men, scarcely beyond boyhood, having with them a horse and a mule. They stopped not far from us, turned out their animals to feed, made a fire and took their evening meal, as we were doing; and, after awhile, came over to our camp to talk. They also had launched out alone, and would be very glad to keep in company with us. As they appeared civil, and one of them rather gentlemanly, we of course did not object. This seemed like a little more protection; but it had its drawbacks; for we soon found out they had very little to eat; and in a few days they began to plead for some of our flour; promising they would hunt, away from the road, every day and bring in game to keep up the supply of provisions. But game was scarce, and very few were the times along the whole way that they caught any. We had allowed a very small margin of provisions for contingencies, because the necessity for the fastest possible traveling was so great.

Still we kept on, sharing, and hoping for the best. Their efforts at hunting, fruitless as they usually were, kept the young men away from the road most of the time, so that we were nearly as much alone as ever. On the morning of the 11th of September they had been away from us for some hours. We were moving quietly along our way, no living creature, save our plodding team and our own feeble company, within sight, when, suddenly, there appeared from between the hills a party of Indians. As they came nearer we saw they were all

armed; and presently several arranged themselves in a
sort of semi-circle closing the road, and one of them
laid his rifle across the foreheads of our leaders, and
stopped the team.

[*The Indians of the arid Central Basin were the de-
spised Diggers, a weak people who had been driven into
the desert by more powerful neighbors. Since no large
animals were to be had, the Diggers were forced in times
of stress to a diet of roots and reptiles. In winter they
sought shelter from icy winds in semicircular wickiups
of brush without roofs. Chronically harried by more
powerful tribes and, later, by white men, they were a
cowardly race almost as fleet in running away as their
chief game animal, the rabbit. In the summer of 1849
many of them hid along the trail of the gold-seekers to
pilfer when opportunity offered and sometimes to toma-
hawk a lone hunter. The rifles possessed by the band
threatening the Royce party were, no doubt, obtained
in one way or another from white fur traders.*]

From my seat in the wagon I had from their first appearance observed every movement. I saw we were completely in their power. Their numbers and their arms
were enough to destroy us in a few moments. Even if
the young men with their guns were at hand there would
be no hope in battle. If firing once commenced those
savages would not cease till they had laid low, at least
every man of the company. There was no hope, save in
an influence that should change their purpose, in so far
as it was hostile, and supply motives for letting us go.
With my whole soul I prayed that God would wield that
influence, and supply those motives; and as they closed
around us I cast all into His hands without any other
hope.

At first every appearance was hostile. They were importunate in demanding various things, acted with the air of victors, some of the younger ones pressed close to the wagon, and looked in, with boisterous exclamations and impertinent gestures. But I was enabled to keep a firm unblenching front, taking care that my little Mary did not stir from my side. She was too young to realize any danger, and thought the whole rather amusing. My husband met them from the first with a calm, business-like air, as if he thought they wanted to hold a consultation with him; and when they became overbearing, he still kept on making speeches to them, though we could not perceive that they understood what he said. Their behavior changed several times quite strangely. They would draw nearer together and consult with puzzled looks, some of them still guarding the team. Then they would scowl and seem to differ among themselves. Thus they kept us for perhaps an hour, when, all at once, my husband raised the big ox-whip, shouted to the cattle, and rushed them forward so suddenly that those nearest Indians instinctively stepped aside, then pompously exclaiming "I'm going to move on" he called the old man to follow, and we were once more in motion. But would they let us keep on? I looked through a small gap in the wagon. They were evidently puzzled by such unusual behavior, and as evidently divided in their counsels. Some were vociferating—with their guns in threatening positions—others plainly differed from them, but it was certain they had not quite decided what to do, when a turn of the road took us out of sight.

We expected they would way-lay us again; for we were passing through several narrow defiles that day—

but the hours went by and night came, without another sight of the enemy. My husband kept guard that night, and I slept very little. The others of our little company disappeared among the bushes and seemed to sleep as well as usual.

Two days after this we met a band of Mormons who had been gold-hunting in California for the summer, and were on their return to Salt Lake. This was the company whose leader was to tell us how we might get from the Sink of the Humboldt, otherwise Mary's River, to Carson River; for that was a part of our journey which yet lay shrouded in grim mystery. The directions given us seemed very plain. He traced out the road in the sand with a stick—I think it was his whip handle. It was taken for granted that we knew our way to the "Sink of the Mary's [Humboldt] River" so he took *that* for his starting point in giving us directions, and showed us that, soon after passing there, we would see a plain wagon track leading to the left, which we were to follow, and it would bring us to grassy meadows, lying two or three miles from the main road, and so, still abounding in feed. Here also, he said, we would find several shallow wells, dug but recently—in the last part of the season—by Mormons, who had gone to spend the winter in California, and on their way there had found these meadows, cut feed in them for use on the forty mile desert and, on arriving in California had given to him and his company—then just about to start for Salt Lake—directions to find the spot. The wells, he said had good water in them when he was there a few days before. None of them were deep, but the water was near the surface all about there, and we could, if we found it desirable, scoop out one or two of the holes deeper, let them settle all night, and in the morning have plenty of fresh water.

He was evidently an old and experienced traveler of deserts, plains and mountains. He advised us to camp in the meadows he described, for at least two or three days, let the cattle rest and feed freely, while the men made it their first business to cut as much hay as there was room for in the wagon. This would partly dry while the cattle were recruiting; then load it up, fill every available vessel with water, and set out on the desert about noon of the day, if the weather were cool—otherwise toward evening. When once out on the desert we were to stop at intervals of a few hours, feed some of the hay to the cattle, give them a moderate drink, let them breathe a short time and then go on. In this way, he said, we would be able to reach Carson River in about twenty-four hours from the time of starting on the desert.

After hearing his instructions, and having the road made thus plain to us, we went on with renewed cheerfulness and energy. On Sunday the 16th of September we camped on the head branch of Mary's River, and on Monday morning passed through a cañon which brought us to the River itself, down which we continued to travel for several days. It was now getting late in the season, and we could not help feeling it rather ominous that a thunder-storm overtook us one evening followed by cold nights; and on the evening and night of the 1st of October a terrific wind blew, threatening for hours to strangle us with thick clouds of sand, and to blow our wagon, with all our means of living, over the steep bluff. But a good Providence preserved us and, with the morning calm returned. We had now nearly reached the head

of Humboldt Lake, which, at this late period in the dry
season, was utterly destitute of water, the river having
sunk gradually in the sand, until, hereabout it entirely
disappeared. Still, the name, "Sink of Mary's or Humboldt River" was applied in our Guide Book, as well as
in conversations at Salt Lake City, to the *southern* or
lower end of Humboldt Lake, a point some ten miles
farther on our way, where, we were told, there were
several holes dug, close to the road. Having always
understood it to be thus applied, it of course never came
into our minds to suppose, that our Mormon friend,
when he so particularly marked in the sand "The Sink
of Mary's," meant the point where at that time the
river actually disappeared.

When, therefore, on the night of October 2nd, we
camped in the neighborhood of the last mentioned point,
we said, "Now, we must be about twelve or thirteen
miles from where that road to the meadows leads off to
the left; and thence it will be only two or three miles to
the meadows, where we are to rest and prepare for the
desert. If we rise *very* early tomorrow morning, we shall
get there by noon, and have a half day to settle camp,
and get ready for work." Accordingly the first one
who woke the next morning roused all the rest, and,
though we found it was not much past two o'clock, we
agreed it was not best to sleep again; so, by our fire of
sage-brush we took some hot coffee, and the last bit of
rabbit pot-pie—the result of a very rare success the day
before—yoked up the oxen, and went resolutely on our
way.

It was moonlight, but the gray-white sand with only
here and there a sage-brush looked all so much alike
that it required care to keep the road. And now, for

the first time in my life, I saw a mirage; or several repetitions of that optical illusion. Once it was an extended sheet of water lying calmly bright in the moonlight, with here and there a tree on its shores; and our road seemed to tend directly towards it; then it was a small lake seen through openings in a row of trees, while the shadowy outlines of a forest appeared beyond it; all lying to our left. What a pity it seemed to be passing it by, when our poor animals had been so stinted of late. Again, we were traveling parallel with a placid river on our right; beyond which were trees; and from us to the water's edge the ground sloped so gently it appeared absurd not to turn aside to its brink and refresh ourselves and our oxen.

But, as day dawned, these beautiful sights disappeared, and we began to look anxiously for the depression in the ground, and the holes dug, which we were told would mark the Sink of the Humboldt. But it was nearly noonday before we came to them. There was still some passable water in the holes, but not fit to drink clear, so we contrived to gather enough sticks of sage to boil some, made a little coffee, ate our lunch and, thus refreshed, we hastened to find the forking road. Our director had told us, that within about two or three miles beyond the Sink we might look for the road, to the left, and we did look, and kept looking, and going on, drearily, till the sun got lower and lower, and night was fast approaching. Then the conviction, which had long been gaining ground in my mind, took possession of the whole party. We had passed the forks of the road before daylight, that morning, and were now miles out on the desert without a mouthful of food for the cattle and only two or three quarts of water in a little cask.

What could be done? Halt we must, for the oxen were nearly worn out and night was coming on. The animals must at least rest, if they could not be fed: and, that they might rest, they were chained securely to the wagon, for, hungry and thirsty as they were, they would, if loose, start off frantically in search of water and food, and soon drop down exhausted. Having fastened them in such a way that they could lie down, we took a few mouthfuls of food, and then, we in our wagon and the men not far off upon the sand, fell wearily to sleep; a forlorn little company wrecked upon the desert.

The first question in the morning was, "How can the oxen be kept from starving?" A happy thought occurred. We had, thus far on our journey, managed to keep something in the shape of a bed to sleep on. It was a mattress-tick, and, just before leaving Salt Lake, we had put into it some fresh hay—not very much, for our load must be as light as possible; but the old gentleman traveling with us had also a small straw mattress; the two together might keep the poor things from starving for a few hours. At once a small portion was dealt out to them and for the present they were saved. For ourselves we had food which we believed would about last us till we reached the Gold Mines if we could go right on: if we were much delayed anywhere, it was doubtful. The two or three quarts of water in our little cask would last only a few hours, to give moderate drinks to each of the party. For myself I inwardly determined I should scarcely take any of it as, I had found, throughout the journey, that I could do with less drink than most land travelers. Some of the men, however, easily suffered with thirst, and, as to my little girl, it is well known, a child cannot do long without either water or milk. Everything looked rather dark, and dubious.

Should we try to go on? But there were miles of desert before us, in which, we knew, neither grass or water could be found. We had been told by those who had crossed it with comparatively fresh teams, that, with plenty of hay and water to bait with, we might get over it in about twenty-four hours, though it was acknowledged it might take us longer. Here we were, without water, and with only a few mouthfuls of poor feed, while our animals were already tired out, and very hungry and thirsty. No, it would be madness to go farther out in the desert under such conditions. Should we then turn back and try to reach the meadows with their wells? But, as near as we could calculate, it could not be less than twelve or fifteen miles to them. Would it be possible for our poor cattle to reach there? Their only food would be that pitiful mess still left in our mattresses. It might be divided into two portions, giving them each a few mouthfuls more at noon, and then, if they kept on their feet long enough to reach the holes at the Sink, we might possibly find enough water to give them each a little drink, which, with the remainder of the fodder might keep them up till the meadows were reached. It was a forlorn hope; but it was all we had.

The morning was wearing away while these things were talked over. Precious time was being wasted; but, the truth was, the situation was so new and unexpected, that it seemed for awhile to confuse—almost to stupefy —most of the little party; and, those least affected in this way, felt so deeply the responsibility of the next move, that they dared not decide upon it hastily. The least responsible and efficient of the company had been most of the morning, wandering aimlessly about, sometimes keeping within a small circle, then again branching off nearly out of sight. Perhaps they all had a vague hope they might find another track. But now, as noon approached, they gathered near the wagon, tired, moody, and evidently very near "giving up." But this would never do. So the more hopeful ones proposed that we should all eat something and, as soon as the noon heat abated, prepare for a move. So we took some lunch, and soon the men were lying upon the sand at short distances from each other, fast asleep. My little Mary slept too. But I was not sleepy. With unwearied gaze my eyes swept, again and again, the shimmering horizon. There was no help or hope there. Then I looked at what lay nearest. How short-lived our few remaining resources would be, unless fresh strength came soon from somewhere. How still it was. Only the sound of a few feeble breaths. It would not take many hours of starvation to quiet them forever.

All the human aid we had could do but little now; and if, in trying to do that little, one more mistake were made, it must be fatal. Whence then this calm strength which girded me round so surely, while I, and all surrounding me were so weak? I had known what it was to *believe* in God, and to pray that He would never leave us. Was it thus then, that when all other helpers failed, He came so near that I no longer simply *believed* in Him, but *knew* His presence there, giving strength for whatever might come? Soon some of the party awoke and, after a little talk, concluded that two of them would walk to a bald ridge that rose out of the flat waste, about a mile and a half distant, and take a view from thence, in the faint hope that we might yet be mis-

taken, and the forking road and the meadows might still
be in advance. My husband said he would go, and the
best of the two young men went with him, while the
other two wandered listlessly off again. I made no opposition; I felt no inclination to oppose; though I knew
the helplessness and loneliness of the position would
thus be greatly increased. But that calm strength, that
certainty of One near and all sufficient hushed and
cheered me. Only a woman who has been alone upon a
desert with her helpless child can have any adequate
idea of my experience for the next hour or two. But
that consciousness of an unseen Presence still sustained
me.

When the explorers returned from their walk to the
ridge, it was only to report, no discovery: nothing to
be seen on all sides but sand and scattered sagebrush
interspersed with the carcasses of dead cattle. So there
was nothing to be done but to turn back and try to find
the meadows. Turn back! What a chill the words sent
through one. *Turn back*, on a journey like that; in
which every mile had been gained by most earnest labor,
growing more and more intense, until, of late, it had
seemed that the certainty of *advance* with every step,
was all that made the next step possible. And now for
miles we were to *go back*. In all that long journey no
steps ever seemed so heavy, so hard to take, as those
with which I turned my back to the sun that afternoon
of October 4th, 1849.

We had not been long on the move when we saw dust
rising in the road at a distance, and soon perceived we
were about to meet a little caravan of wagons. Then a
bright gleam of hope stole in. They had doubtless
stopped at the meadows, and were supplied with grass

and water. Might it not be possible that they would have enough to spare for us? Then we could go on with them. My heart bounded at the thought. But the hope was short lived. We met, and some of the men gathered round our wagon with eager inquiries, while those who could not leave their teams stood looking, with wonder, at a solitary wagon headed the wrong way.

Our story was soon told. It turned out that they were camping in the meadows at the very time we passed the forking road without seeing it, the morning we so ambitiously started soon after midnight. Ah, we certainly got up too early that day. If we had only seen that road and taken it, we might now have been with this company, provided for the desert, and no longer alone. But, when the question was asked whether they could spare sufficient grass and water to get our team over the desert, they shook their heads, and unanimously agreed that it was out of the question. Their own cattle, they said, were weak from long travel and too often scant supplies. They had only been able to load up barely enough to get to the Carson River. The season was far advanced and the clouds, hanging of late round the mountain tops, looked threatening. It would be like throwing away their own lives without any certainty of saving ours; for once out in the desert without food we would all be helpless together. One of the men had his family with him, a wife and two or three children; and while they talked the woman was seen coming towards us. She had not, when they first halted, understood that any but men were with the lone wagon. As soon as she heard to the contrary, and what were the circumstances, she hastened, with countenance full of concern, to condole with me; and, I think, had the decision depended alone upon her, she would have insisted upon our turning back with them and sharing their feed and water to the last.

But fortunately for them, probably for us all, other counsels prevailed, and we resumed our depressing backward march. Two or three things, before uncertain, were settled by this meeting. The first was the distance to the meadows, which they agreed could not be less than fourteen or sixteen miles from where we met them, which seemed, in our circumstances, like an appalling interval. But there was relief in being assured that we should find a pretty good supply of water in the holes at the Sink, where we were to camp that night, and that, when we once reached the meadows, there was food and water enough for a number of teams during many days. We had also definite directions as to the shortest road, and were assured it was perfectly plain, and good except that it was rather sandy.

I had now become so impressed with the danger of the cattle giving out, that I refused to ride except for occasional brief rests. So, soon after losing sight of the dust of the envied little caravan, I left the wagon and walked the remainder of the day. For a good while I kept near the wagon but, by and by, being very weary I fell behind. The sun had set, before we reached the Sink, and the light was fading fast when the wagon disappeared from my sight behind a slight elevation; and, as the others had gone on in advance some time before, I was all alone on the barren waste. However, as I recognized the features of the neighborhood, and knew we were quite near the Sink, I felt no particular apprehension, only a feeling that it was a weird and dreary scene and instinctively urged forward my lagging footsteps in hope of regaining sight of the wagon.

Suddenly I caught sight of an object a few rods distant on the left of the road, moving steadily but rather stealthily toward the road, in a line that would intercept it some paces ahead of me. I stopped—the creature stopped too, looking steadily at me. It was a coyote. I had several times during the journey heard them howling at night but, as the season had advanced, they had been seldom heard, and to meet one thus almost face to face with no human being in sight was a little startling. But, calling to mind what I had heard of their reluctance to face a steady look and determined resistance, I lifted my hands with threatening gestures, raised a shout, and sprang forward a step or two. Mr. Coyote stood a moment as if questioning the resistance offered; but when I repeated, more violently, the gestures and the shouts, he turned and retraced his steps into the dim distance, only looking back once or twice to see if the enemy retained the ground. As he disappeared I hastened forward, and in a few minutes came within sight of the wagon, now halted for the night near the camp fire, which the men had just lit.

The next morning we resumed our backward march after feeding out the last mouthful of fodder. The water in the little cask was nearly used up in making coffee for supper and breakfast; but, if only each one would be moderate in taking a share when thirst impelled him, we might yet reach the wells before any one suffered seriously. We had lately had but few chances for cooking; and only a little boiled rice with dried fruit, and a few bits of biscuit remained after we had done break-

fast. If we could only reach the meadows by noon. But
that we could hardly hope for, the animals were so weak
and tired. There was no alternative, however, the only
thing to be done was to go steadily on, determined to
do and endure to the utmost.

I found no difficulty this morning in keeping up with
the team. They went so slowly, and I was so preternatu-
rally stimulated by anxiety to get forward, that, before I was aware of it I would be some rods ahead of the
cattle, straining my gaze as if expecting to see a land
of promise, long before I had any rational hope of the
kind. My imagination acted intensely. I seemed to see
Hagar, in the wilderness walking wearily away from
her fainting child among the dried up bushes, and seat-
ing herself in the hot sand. I seemed to become Hagar
myself, and when my little one, from the wagon behind
me, called out, "Mamma I want a drink"—I stopped,
gave her some, noted that there were but a few swallows
left, then mechanically pressed onward again, alone, repeating, over and over, the words, "Let me not see the
death of the child."

Just in the heat of noon-day we came to where the
sage bushes were nearer together; and a fire, left by
campers or Indians, had spread for some distance, leaving beds of ashes, and occasionally charred skeletons of
bushes to make the scene more dreary. Smoke was still
sluggishly curling up here and there, but no fire was
visible; when suddenly just before me to my right a
bright flame sprang up at the foot of a small bush, ran
rapidly up it, leaped from one little branch to another
till all, for a few seconds, were ablaze together, then
went out, leaving nothing but a few ashes and a little
smouldering trunk. It was a small incident, easily ac-

counted for, but to my then over-wrought fancy it made more vivid the illusion of being a wanderer in a far off, old time desert, and myself witnessing a wonderful phenomenon. For a few moments I stood with bowed head worshiping the God of Horeb, and I was strengthened thereby.

Wearily passed the hottest noon-day hour, with many an anxious look at the horned-heads, which seemed to me to bow lower and lower, while the poor tired hoofs almost refused to move. The two young men had been out of sight for sometime; when, all at once, we heard a shout, and saw, a few hundred yards in advance a couple of hats thrown into the air and four hands waving triumphantly. As soon as we got near enough, we heard them call out, "Grass and water! Grass and water!" and shortly we were at the meadows. The remainder of that day was spent chiefly in rest and refreshment. The next day the men busied themselves in cutting and spreading grass; while I sorted out and re-arranged things in the wagon so as to make all possible room for hay and water; and also cooked all the meat we had left, and as much of our small stock of flour, rice, and dried fruits, as might last us till we could again find wood.

The day after that was Sunday, and we should have had a very quiet rest, had we not been visited by a party of some eight or ten Indians, who came from the Humboldt Mountains on Saturday afternoon, and remained near us till we left. They professed to be friendly; but were rather troublesome, and evidently desirous of getting something out of us if they could. Two or three of them had rifles; and when the young men went to talk to them they began to show off their marksmanship by

firing at particular objects. The young men felt this to
be rather of the nature of a challenge; and thought it
would be safer to accept than to ignore it. So they got
the arms from the wagon, set up a mark, and, as one of
them—the gentleman of the two—proved to be a remarkable shot, the Indians were struck with surprise,
which, as, time after time, W——'s ball hit within an
inch of his aim, grew to admiration, and ended in evident awe; for not one of their party could quite equal
him. How much our safety, and exemption from pillage
were due to that young man's true aim we might not
be quite sure; but I have always been very willing to
acknowledge a debt of gratitude to him.

On Monday morning we loaded up, but did not hurry,
for the cattle had not rested any too long; another day
would have been better; but we dared not linger. So,
giving them time that morning thoroughly to satisfy
themselves with grass and water we once more set forward toward the formidable desert, and, at that late
season, with our equipment, the scarcely less formidable
Sierras. The feeling that we were once more going forward instead of backward, gave an animation to every
step which we could never have felt but by contrast. By
night we were again at the Sink where we once more
camped; but we durst not, the following morning,
launch out upon the desert with the whole day before
us; for, though it was now the 9th of October, the sun
was still powerful for some hours daily, and the arid
sand doubled its heat. Not much after noon, however,
we ventured out upon the sea of sand; this time to cross
or die.

Not far from the edge of night we stopped to bait, at
no great distance from the scene of our last week's bit-

ter disappointment. Once beyond that, I began to feel renewed courage, as though the worst were passed; and, as I had walked much of the afternoon, and knew I must walk again by and by, I was persuaded to get into the wagon and lie down by Mary, who was sleeping soundly. By a strong effort of will, backed by the soothing influence of prayer, I fell asleep, but only for a few minutes. I was roused by the stopping of the wagon, and then my husband's voice said, "So you've given out, have you Tom?" and at the same moment I knew by the rattling chains and yokes that some of the cattle were being loosed from the team. I was out of the wagon in a minute. One of the oxen was prostrate on the ground, and his companion, from whose neck the yoke was just being removed, looked very likely soon to follow him. It had been the weak couple all along. Now we had but two yoke. How soon would they, one by one, follow?

Nothing could induce me to get into the wagon again. I said I would walk by the team, and for awhile I did; but by and by I found myself yards ahead. An inward power urged me forward; and the poor cattle were so slow, it seemed every minute as if they were going to stop. When I got so far off as to miss the sound of footsteps and wheels, I would pause, startled, wait and listen, dreading lest they had stopped, then as they came near, I would again walk beside them awhile, watching, through the darkness, the dim outlines of their heads and horns to see if they drooped lower. But soon I found myself again forward and alone. There was no moon yet, but by starlight we had for some time seen, only too plainly, the dead bodies of cattle lying here and there on both sides of the road. As we advanced they increased in numbers, and presently we saw two or three wagons. At first we thought we had overtaken a company, but coming close, no sign of life appeared. We had candles with us, so, as there was not the least breeze, we lit one or two and examined. Everything indicated a complete break down, and a hasty flight. Some animals were lying nearly in front of a wagon, apparently just as they had dropped down, while loose yokes and chains indicated that part of the teams had been driven on, laden probably with some necessaries of life; for the contents of the wagons were scattered in confusion, the most essential articles alone evidently having been thought worth carrying. "Ah," we said, "some belated little company has been obliged to pack what they could, and hurry to the river. Maybe it was the little company we met the other day." It was not a very encouraging scene but our four oxen still kept their feet; we would drive on a little farther, out of this scene of ruin, bait them, rest ourselves and go on. We did so, but soon found that what we had supposed an exceptional misfortune must have been the common fate of many companies; for at still shortening intervals, scenes of ruin similar to that just described kept recurring till we seemed to be but the last, little, feeble, struggling band at the rear of a routed army.

From near midnight, on through the small hours, it appeared necessary to stop more frequently, for both man and beast were sadly weary, and craved frequent nourishment. Soon after midnight we finished the last bit of meat we had; but there was still enough of the biscuit, rice and dried fruit to give us two or three more little baits. The waning moon now gave us a little melancholy light, showing still the bodies of dead cattle, and the forms of forsaken wagons as our grim way-marks. In one or two instances they had been left in the very middle of the road; and we had to turn out into the untracked sand to pass them. Soon we came upon a scene of wreck that surpassed anything preceding it. As we neared it, we wondered at the size of the wagons, which, in the dim light, looked tall as houses, against the sky. Coming to them, we found three or four of them to be of the make that the early Mississippi Valley emi-grants used to call "Prairie Schooners": having deep beds, with projecting backs and high tops. One of them was specially immense, and, useless as we felt it to be to spend time in examining these warning relics of those who had gone before us, curiosity led us to lift the front curtain, which hung down, and by the light of our can-dle that we had again lit, look in. There from the strong, high bows, hung several sides of well cured ba-con, much better in quality than that we had finished, at our last resting place. So we had but a short interval in which to say we were destitute of meat, for, though, warned by all we saw not to add a useless pound to our load, we thought it wise to take a little, to eke out our scanty supply of food. And, as to the young men, who had so rarely, since they joined us, had a bit of meat they could call their own, they were very glad to bear the burden of a few pounds of bacon slung over their shoulders.

After this little episode, the only cheering incident for many hours, we turned to look at what lay round these monster wagons. It would be impossible to de-scribe the motley collection of things of various sorts, strewed all about. The greater part of the materials, however, were pasteboard boxes, some complete, but most of them broken, and pieces of wrapping paper still creased, partially in the form of packages. But the most prominent objects were two or three, perhaps more, very beautifully finished trunks of various sizes, some of them standing open, their pretty trays lying on the ground, and all rifled of their contents; save that occasionally a few pamphlets, or, here and there, a book remained in the corners. We concluded that this must have been a company of merchants hauling a load of goods to California, that some of their animals had given out, and, fearing the rest would they had packed such things as they could, and had fled for their lives toward the river. There was only one thing, (besides the few pounds of bacon) that, in all these varied heaps of things, many of which, in civilized scenes, would have been valuable, I thought worth picking up. That was a little book, bound in cloth and illustrated with a number of small engravings. Its title was "Little Ella." I thought it would please Mary, so I put it in my pocket. It was an easily carried souvenir of the desert; and more than one pair of young eyes learned to read its pages in after years.

Morning was now approaching, and we hoped, when full daylight came, to see some signs of the river. But, for two or three weary hours after sunrise nothing of the kind appeared. The last of the water had been given to the cattle before daylight. When the sun was up we gave them the remainder of their hay, took a little breakfast and pressed forward. For a long time not a word was spoken save occasionally to the cattle. I had again, unconsciously, got in advance; my eyes scanning the horizon to catch the first glimpse of any change;

though I had no definite idea in my mind what first to expect. But now there was surely something. Was it a cloud? It was very low at first and I feared it might evaporate as the sun warmed it. But it became rather more distinct and a little higher. I paused, and stood till the team came up. Then walking beside it I asked my husband what he thought that low dark line could be. "I think," he said, "it must be the timber on Carson River." Again we were silent and for a while I watched anxiously the heads of the two leading cattle. They were rather unusually fine animals, often showing considerable intelligence, and so faithful had they been, through so many trying scenes, I could not help feeling a sort of attachment to them; and I pitied them, as I observed how low their heads drooped as they pressed their shoulders so resolutely and yet so wearily against the bows. Another glance at the horizon. Surely there was now visible a little unevenness in the top of that dark line, as though it might indeed be trees. "How far off do you think that is now?" I said. "About five or six miles I guess," was the reply. At that moment the white-faced leader raised his head, stretched forward his nose and uttered a low "Moo-o-oo." I was startled fearing it was the sign for him to fall, exhausted. "What is the matter with him?" I said. "I think he smells the water" was the answer. "How can he at such a distance?" As I spoke, the other leader raised his head, stretched out his nose, and uttered the same sound. The hinder cattle seemed to catch the idea, whatever it was; they all somewhat increased their pace, and from that time, showed renewed animation.

But we had yet many weary steps to take, and noon had passed before we stood in the shade of those longed-for trees, beside the Carson River. As soon as the yokes were removed the oxen walked into the stream, and stood a few moments, apparently enjoying its coolness, then drank as they chose, came out, and soon found feed that satisfied them for the present, though at this point it was not abundant. The remainder of that day was spent in much needed rest. The next day we did not travel many miles, for our team showed decided signs of weakness, and the sand became deeper as we advanced, binding the wheels so as to make hauling very hard. We had conquered the desert.

CHAPTER III

Mountains

It remains for the individual experience to show to us, if it can, the presence of our Deliverer, the coming of that which we shall recognise as divine, just because it truly and authoritatively reveals to the Self the fulfilment that we need, by bringing us into touch with the real nature of things. We need to find the presence that can give this unity and self-possession to the soul. . . . Our individual experience must become some sort of intercourse with Another. And this Other must be in some sense the Master of Life, the Might that overcometh the world, the revealer of final truth. . . . Is such a direct touch with the divine possible? The mystics of all ages have maintained that it is possible. Are they right?

JOSIAH ROYCE, *Sources of Religious Insight.*

Mountains

[*The Royce party stood at the eastern base of the vast uptilted granite block which is the Sierra Nevada range. The immigrant trail climbed steeply to high notches. The season was dangerously late. Already in the uplands winter gales were filling the ravines with snow. Only haste and good fortune could save the party. They pressed on realizing their danger.*]

BUT the great Sierra Nevada Mountains were still all before us, and we had many miles to make, up this [Carson] River, before their ascent was fairly begun. If this sand continued many miles as looked probable, when should we ever even begin the real climbing? The men began to talk among themselves about how much easier they could get on if they left the wagon; and it was not unlikely they would try starting out without us, if we had to travel too slowly. But they could not do this to any real advantage unless they took with them their pack-mule to carry some provisions. All they had was the bacon they found on the desert, and some parched corn meal; but they felt sanguine that they could go so much faster than the cattle with the wagon, they could easily make this last them through. But the bargain had been, when we agreed to supply them with flour, that the pack mule, and the old horse if he could be of any use, should be at our service to aid in any pinch that might occur, to the end of the journey. Having shared the perils of the way thus far, it certainly seemed unwise to divide the strength of so small a party when the mountains were to be scaled.

I wished most heartily there was some more rapid way for Mary and me to ride. But it was out of the question; for only a thoroughly trained mountain animal would do for me to ride carrying her. Besides this, all the clothing and personal conveniences we had in the world were in our wagon, and we had neither a sufficient number of sound animals nor those of the right kind, to pack them across the mountains. So the only way was to try to keep on. But it looked like rather a hopeless case when, for this whole day, we advanced but a few miles.

The next morning, Friday the 12th of October, we set out once more, hoping the sand would become lighter and the road easier to travel. But, instead of this, the wheels sank deeper than yesterday, there was more of ascent to overcome, the sun shone out decidedly hot, and, towards noon, we saw that we were approaching some pretty steep hills up which our road evidently led. It did not look as though we could ascend them but we would at least try to reach their foot. As we neared them we saw dust rising from the road at one of the turns we could distinguish high up in the hills a few miles off. Probably it was some party ahead of us. There was no hope of our overtaking anybody, so when we lost sight of the dust we did not expect to see it again. But soon another section of the road was in sight, and again the dust appeared; this time nearer, and plainly moving toward us. Conjecture now became very lively. It was probably Indians; but they could not be of the same tribes we had seen. Were they foes? How many were there? Repeatedly we saw the dust at different points, but could make out no distinct figures.

We were now so near the foot of the hills that we

could distinctly see a stretch of road leading down a very steep incline to where we were moving so laboriously along. Presently at the head of this steep incline appeared two horsemen, clad in loose, flying garments that flapped, like wings on each side of them, while their broad-brimmed hats blown up from their foreheads, revealed hair and faces that belonged to no Indians. Their rapidity of motion and the steepness of the descent gave a strong impression of coming down from above, and the thought flashed into my mind, "They look heaven-sent." As they came nearer we saw that each of them led by a halter a fine mule, and the perfect ease with which all the animals cantered down that steep, was a marvel in our eyes. My husband and myself were at the heads of the lead cattle, and our little Mary was up in the front of the wagon, looking with wonder at the approaching forms.

As they came near they smiled and the forward one said "Well sir, you are the man we are after!" "How can that be?" said my husband, with surprise. "Yes, sir," continued the stranger, "you and your wife, and that little girl, are what brought us as far as this. You see we belong to the Relief Company sent out by order of the United States Government to help the late emigrants over the mountains. We were ordered only as far as Truckee Pass. When we got there we met a little company that had just got in. They'd been in a snow storm at the summit; 'most got froze to death themselves, lost some of their cattle, and just managed to get to where some of our men had fixed a relief camp. There was a woman and some children with them; and that woman set right to work at us fellows to go on over the mountains after a family she said they'd met on the desert going back for grass and water 'cause they'd missed their way. She said there was only one wagon, and there was a woman and child in it; and she knew they could never get through them cañons and over them ridges without help. We told her we had no orders to go any farther then. She said she didn't care for orders. She didn't believe anybody would blame us for doing what we were sent out to do, if we did have to go farther than ordered. And she kept at me so, I couldn't get rid of her. You see I've got a wife and little girl of my own; so I felt just how it was; and I got this man to come with me and here we are, to give you more to eat, if you want it, let you have these two mules, and tell you how to get right over the mountains the best and quickest way."

While he thus rapidly, in cheery though blunt fashion, explained their sudden presence with us, the thought of their being heaven-sent—that had so lightly flashed into my mind as I at first watched their rapid descent of the hill, with flying garments—grew into a sweetly solemn conviction; and I stood in mute adoration, breathing, in my inmost heart, thanksgiving to that Providential Hand which had taken hold of the conflicting movements, the provoking blunders, the contradictory plans, of our lives and those of a dozen other people, who a few days before were utterly unknown to each other, and many miles apart, and had from those rough, broken materials wrought out for us so unlooked for a deliverance.

Having made their hasty explanation, our new friends advised us to keep on some little distance farther, to a point where there was a spring in the hills, and excellent camping, to which they would guide us.

There we were to rest the remainder of the day, while they would help to select, put into proper shape and pack, everything in the wagon that could be packed. The rest we must be content to leave. As we moved leisurely on to our camping place, they explained more fully the details of our situation—which they understood so much better than we could—and told us what we were to do. There had been two nights of snow storm at the summit: had there come much more they could not have got through. But the weather had cleared, the snow was fast going off the roads as they came over; and, if no other storm occurred, the pass would be in good order when we reached it. But we must hasten with all possible despatch, for, when the storms once again set in, they were not likely at that season to give any more chance for crossing the mountains. As to keeping on with the wagon, even supposing the cattle to grow no weaker than now,—it would take us two weeks at the least to ascend the Carson Valley to the cañon. That cañon could not in several places be traversed by wheels. Wagons had been taken through; but only by taking them apart and packing, at the most difficult points; which of course could only be done by strong companies with plenty of time. Our only hope, therefore, was to pack. They then went farther into details about packing. The oxen, they said, could easily be made to carry, each, two moderate sized bundles, if snugly packed and well fastened on. Then the old horse could carry something though not very much. And the mule the young men had brought along, they said must carry most of the provisions.

"And now as to these two mules we brought," continued the chief speaker, "this white one is a perfectly-trained, mountain saddle-mule. My wife has rode him for miles, over steep and slippery roads, and he'll be perfectly safe for this lady to ride, with her little girl in front of her. And this dark mule is just as good for carrying packs, and the lady is to have him for her things and the little girl's. Now," he continued, turning to me, "as soon as we stop, and have all had some dinner, you just pick out all the things you care most about, and put them by themselves—you can save out enough for two good sized packs: he's strong, and understands it—and we'll do them up snug for you, and show the men how to fasten them on safe; and you remember, now, that these two mules are yours till you get through to the gold-mines; and all Uncle Sam asks, is, that they shall be brought safely to his boys' headquarters in Sacramento City as soon as possible after you get into California."

Thus, by the wise forethought of our good Government, and the chivalrous management of this faithful agent, I was provided for to a sufficiency that would have looked to me, two hours before, like a fairy-dream. The programme for the afternoon was successfully carried out. Every thing was arranged for an early morning start; and, at night I lay down to sleep for the last time in the wagon that had proved such a shelter for months past. I remembered well, how dreary it had seemed, on the first night of our journey (which now looked so long ago) to have *only* a *wagon* for shelter. Now we were not going to have even that. But, never mind, if we might only reach in safety the other foot of the mountains, all these privations would in their turn look small; and the same rich Providence that had led, and was still so kindly leading us, would, in that new

land, perhaps, show us better things than we had seen
yet.

So, when morning came, I hailed it with cheerful
hope, though with some misgivings, because I had not
ridden horseback for several years, and, whenever I had,
it had been with side-saddle, and all the usual equip-
ments for lady's riding, and, certainly, with no baby to
carry. Now, I was to have only a common Spanish
saddle, I must have Mary in front of me, and, it turned
out, that several things needed for frequent use would
have to be suspended from the pommel of my saddle, in
a satchel on one side and a little pail on the other. At
first, I was rather awkward, and so afraid Mary would
get hurt, that at uneven places in the road I would ask
my husband to get up and take her, while I walked. But
in a few hours this awkwardness wore off; and the second day of our new style of traveling I rode twenty-five
miles, only alighting once or twice for a brief time. Our
friends, the government men, had left us the morning we
left our wagon; taking the road to the Truckee, where
they felt themselves emphatically "due," considering
their orders. I have more than once since wished I could
see and thank them again; for, grateful as I felt then,
I was able to appreciate more highly, a thousand fold,
the service they had rendered us when, only ten days
after we crossed the summit, the mountains were all
blocked with snow, and the stormiest winter California
had known for years was fully set in.

About the third day up the Carson, we were overtaken by a small company of men, sent out on some
special business which they did not state, from a western military station; and bound for California. Their
animals were exclusively mules, and they were in every

way fully equipped. They camped near us, and the commander, whom they called Col. J——, seemed much impressed with the defenselessness of our condition. Most of the young men shared this feeling more or less, and behaved very gentlemanly. Of course their animals could travel much faster than ours, so we could not hope to join their company. But Col. J—— suggested that as they had been traveling pretty fast for many days, and the ascent was now becoming more steep, it would be as well for them to make shorter days' rides till the summit was passed; in which case we might, by traveling a little later, camp near them at night, and so be less in danger from Indians. He said they would fire two or three guns when they stopped for the night, so that we might know they were within reach. This was indeed very acceptable aid; and we prized their company still more, when, on coming into camp the second night we found they had, during the afternoon, picked up a man whom they found by the road side, wounded by an Indian arrow. He had wandered off from his party a few days before, looking for game, had lost his way and had only that day regained the road. He was hurrying on alone, when an arrow from a thicket struck him and he fell. The supposition was that the Indians thought him dead, and were prevented from robbery or further violence only by the sudden appearance of Col. J——s company. The wound was painful; but by the good care given him he gradually recovered.

On the 17th of October we reached the head of Carson Valley, and, just after noon, entered the great cañon. Here the road soon became so rough and steep as to make it very difficult for me to hold Mary and keep my seat. The men had hard work to drive the

cattle and mules over the boulders at the frequent crossings of the stream, and in between the great masses of
rock where the trail sometimes almost disappeared. As
the cañon narrowed, the rocky walls towered nearly
perpendicular, hundreds of feet; and seemed in some
places almost to meet above our heads. At some of the
crossings it was well nigh impossible to keep the trail,
so innumerable were the boulders; and the scraggy
bushes so hid the coming-out place. The days were
shortening fast, and, in this deep gulch, darkness began to come on early. The animals became more and
more restive with the roughness of the way, and it was
hard work to keep them from rushing into a narrow ravine that occasionally opened, or up one of the steep
trails which appeared now and then, suggesting unpleasant ideas of Indians and wild beasts. If our animals got many steps away we could not find them in the
dusk.

The young men had lagged behind most of the afternoon, leaving the driving mostly to three of us, one of
whom had to ride, holding the child. Just as the shades
were beginning to make every thing look dim, we came
to a crossing of the creek (which had now become a very
small stream), where on the opposite side instead of the
rocky walls we had had, there was a steep wooded hill
up which wound a trail. But that could not be our way,
for it was too steep, besides we had been told to keep
the cañon, and we thought we could dimly trace *our*
trail, in the sand between the boulders, leading up
stream. We paused to look closely; but the two mules
with their large packs, one containing nearly all the
food of the party, the other the most valuable goods we
possessed, rushed resolutely forward up the creek-bed,

and disappeared among the brush. My husband, who had been carrying Mary for awhile, as I had become tired with the strain, hastily alighted, set her down on a flat rock, told me to take care of my mule for he must follow those animals, and quickly disappeared after them. At the same moment the men came up behind, which started the cattle forward and one of the oxen brushed close by Mary making her fall over into the water. In a moment I was there, had her in my arms, and found she was very little hurt, and her clothes but slightly wet. She was soon soothed; but meanwhile some of the cattle had rushed up the steep trail, and some had scattered among the bushes and boulders all eager to browse. Old Mr. A—— was trying to get together the latter, and young W—— was leading my mule to a convenient place for me to get on, when DeLu who had followed the cattle up the steep trail, called out, "Come on, this is the way!" W—— and the old gentleman both questioned his correctness; but he insisted that the trail became plainer where he was; and when I said I could not ride up so steep a way in the dark, and hold Mary, he said, "O we'll come to an easier part pretty soon, you can get her up here afoot, and W—— can lead up the mule and then you can get on. Come, it's the only way."

Thinking, from his positive tone, that he saw something we could not see W—— and I followed, getting Mary along as well as we could. But, by the time we had climbed awhile, we found the steep growing steeper, and the trail almost disappeared. DeLu stopped, and the two or three cattle who had struggled up, began to tend downward again. It was evident we were lost in the cañon, and had better go no farther in the darkness. I sat down with Mary in my lap, wrapped her closely in

my loose sacque and, feeling it a relief to rest instead of
climb, soothed her and myself as well as I could; looked
at the stars, was thankful there were no signs of storm,
and was conjecturing what had become of my husband
and the mules, when the sound of a gun echoed through
the cañon, followed, soon, by another; and we knew
Col. J——s party were signaling us. The sound came
from the direction in which the mules had disappeared;
and so we hoped they and their driver had arrived at
camp, and would soon send someone to guide us. We
could only account for the lateness of the guns by supposing they had, like ourselves, met with some unusual
adventure, or had forgotten. The young men now called
down to old Mr. A—— to know if he had the other
cattle. He told the number he had been able to get together, and, with those DeLu had, the whole number was
complete. Slowly and with much slipping and sliding,
DeLu now proceeded to get himself and the oxen down
to the creek-bed once more. W—— led my mule in the
same direction; and I followed with Mary, who, instinctively, clung close to my shoulder while I supported her
with my left arm; and, with my right hand took hold of
bushes and branches to break the too rapid descent. I
had not quite reached the bottom when a "Halloa!" was
heard. We answered. From the darkness up the cañon
help soon appeared, we were once more in line of march,
and, in less than an hour, arrived in camp.

The next day we climbed the first of the two ridges
at the summit. And now I realized, in earnest, the value
of a thoroughly trained mountain mule. In several
places the way was so steep that the head of my animal
was even with my eyes as I leaned forward with Mary's
chief weight on my left arm while I clung with my right

hand to the pommel of the saddle, obliged, for the time, to let the mule guide and drive himself. And nobly he did it, never slipping once; while the dark mule did as well with his great load. The other animals had to be driven, urged and kept in the track, while there seemed great danger of their packs being lost or torn; but, near evening, all arrived safely in camp.

That night we slept within a few yards of snow, which lay in a ravine; and water froze in our pans not very far from the fire, which, however, was rather low the last part of the night. But the morning was bright and sunny. "Hope sprang exultant"; for, that day, that blessed 19th of October, we were to cross the highest ridge, view the "promised land," and begin our descent into warmth and safety. So, without flinching I faced steeps still steeper than yesterday: I even laughed in my little one's upturned face, as she lay back against my arm, while I leaned forward almost to the neck of the mule, tugging up the hardest places. I had purposely hastened, that morning, to start ahead of the rest; and not far from noon, I was rewarded by coming out, in advance of all the others, on a rocky height whence I looked, *down*, far over constantly descending hills, to where a soft haze sent up a warm, rosy glow that seemed to me a smile of welcome; while beyond, occasional faint outlines of other mountains appeared; and I knew I was looking across the Sacramento Valley.

California, land of sunny skies—that was my first look into your smiling face. I loved you from that moment, for you seemed to welcome me with loving look into rest and safety. However brave a face I might have put on most of the time, I knew my coward heart was yearning all the while for a home-nest and a welcome into it, and you seemed to promise me both. A short time I had on those rocks, sacred to thanksgiving and prayer; then the others came, and boisterous shouts, and snatches of song made rocks and welkin ring.

We soon began to descend. Not far from the summit, on a small plateau, affording room to camp, and a little timber, we saw traces of fires, and near by, the carcasses of two fine horses evidently not very long dead; while a number of things scattered about looked like hasty flight. We concluded this must have been the scene of disaster of one of those unfortunate parties the relief man had told us of, who were caught in the two nights of snow-storm only about ten days before. And now very cheerily we found our way leading down, and down, and down; so suddenly in some places, that my mule braced his legs and slid. But the next day the descent was not so remarkable; the road became exceedingly dusty; and the spirits of the party flagged somewhat.

We still, each night, made an effort to camp near Col. J—— and his men, for we had been warned that the Indians had in several instances attempted to attack and rob lone emigrants, while still high up in the mountains; though there would be no danger when we reached the mines. On the night of October 21st we unloaded our packs and made our fires within a few rods of our courteous protectors. We had, as usual, made for our own little family a sort of barricade of packs somewhat retired from the others; the men were lying near their fire asleep; and all was still; when a sudden, loud outcry, as of mingled pain and fright followed by other hasty exclamations, and rushing footsteps, and, soon, two or three shots roused us all. We were quickly informed that two Indian arrows had been fired into our neighbors' camp, evidently aimed at the men who were sleeping in the light of their fire. One of the arrows had wounded a man, striking him directly on one of the large ribs, which had prevented its reaching the vitals. The other arrow missed its aim and fell on the ground. Several of the men rushed, armed, into the thicket whence the arrows came, fired, and pursued a short distance. But the enemy knew every turn better than strangers could, and no Indians were to be found. The wounded man proved not to be mortally wounded; and we had the satisfaction of knowing he was improving before we finally parted company—which occurred a day or two after.

On the 24th of October at evening we reached what in our Guide Book was called "Pleasant Valley Gold Mines"; where we found two or three tents, and a few men with their gold-washing pans. They had been at work there for awhile; but said the little "diggings" just there were pretty much "worked out"; and they were going, in a day or two, over to Weaver Creek where, they told us, very fine "prospects had lately been struck," and there was quite a town growing up. That night, we slept, for the first time in several months, without the fear of Indians, or the dread of perils in advance. We rested ourselves and animals for two or three days, and then moved into the village of "Weaverville," of which the miners had told us. This village was made up of tents, many of them very irregularly placed; though in one part, following the trend of the principal ravine, there was, already, something like a row of these primitive dwellings, though at considerable distances apart. We added one to that row, and soon began to gather about us little comforts and conveniences, which made us feel as though we once more had a home. In a few days after we arrived in Weaverville, rain fell heavily, and soon the mountains just above us were blocked by snow. Only one company came through after us; and they barely escaped, by means of good mules. But, with us, lovely, sunny days followed the rainy nights; and, though the season, as a whole, was unusually stormy for California, and doubtless would have been death to any caught at the mountain tops; yet there were intervals that seemed very delightful to those who had spent the preceding winter where the temperature ranged, for many weeks, below zero.

CHAPTER IV
El Dorado

When foreigners accuse us of extraordinary love for gain, and of practical materialism, they fail to see how largely we are a nation of idealists. . . . I am not at all unmindful of that other side—that grosser material side of our national life, upon which our foreign critics so often insist. . . . But you cannot prove the absence of light merely by exploring the darker chasms and caverns of our national existence. Vast as are these recesses of night, the light of large and inspiring ideas shines upon still vaster regions of our American life.

JOSIAH ROYCE, *On Certain Limitations of the Thoughtful Public in America.*

El Dorado

[*After a long summer filled with privations and dangers the Royce family found their journey's end, late in October, in a mining camp. Nerves made taut by the danger of death relaxed. With feelings of relief and gratitude Mrs. Royce sought to reëstablish her home in a community whose only hope of stability lay in the gold in the gravels which underlay it. It was not a community of homes but of unattached men who sojourned within it while their luck was good and who quit it without thought upon news of a new strike elsewhere. In October, 1849, when Mrs. Royce came among them, most of these miners were, as yet, beginners, untrained recruits in the army of gold diggers, who were still living under the influence of the customs and sanctions of the established societies from which they had departed but a few months before. Most of these novices were too busy at the unaccustomed task of cradling gold to realize the possibilities of freedom on the new frontier. Mrs. Royce left her first camp before freedom had evolved into license.*]

AND now began my first experience in a California mining camp. The sense of safety that came from having arrived where there was no danger of attacks from Indians, or of perishing of want or of cold on the desert, or in the mountains, was at first so restful, that I was willing, for awhile, to throw off anxiety; and, like a child fixing a play-house I sang as I arranged our few comforts in our tent. Indeed, part of the time it was fixing a play-house; for Mary was constantly pattering about at my side; and often, things were arranged for her convenience and amusement.

Still, there was a lurking feeling of want of security from having only a cloth wall between us and out of doors. I had heard the sad story (which, while it shocked, reassured us) of the summary punishment inflicted in a neighboring town upon three thieves, who had been tried by a committee of citizens and, upon conviction, all hung. The circumstances had given to the place the name of Hang-Town. We were assured that, since then, no case of stealing had occurred in the northern mines; and I had seen, with my own eyes, buck-skin purses half full of gold-dust, lying on a rock near the road-side, while the owners were working some distance off. So I was not afraid of robbery; but it seemed as if some impertinent person might so easily intrude, or hang about, in a troublesome manner.

But I soon found I had no reason to fear. Sitting in my tent sewing, I heard some men cutting wood up a hill behind us. One of them called out to another "Look out not to let any sticks roll that way, there's a woman and child in that tent." "Aye, aye, we won't frighten them" was the reply, all spoken in pleasant, respectful tones. A number of miners passed every morning and afternoon, to and from their work; but none of them stared obtrusively. One, I observed, looked at Mary with interest a time or two, but did not stop, till one day I happened to be walking with her near the door, when he paused, bowed courteously and said, "Excuse me madam, may I speak to the little girl? We see so few ladies and children in California, and she is about the size of a little sister I left at home." "Certainly," I said, leading her towards him. His gentle tones and pleasant words easily induced her to shake hands, and talk with him. He proved to be a young physician, who had not long commenced practice at home, when the news of gold discovery in California induced him to seek El Dorado, hoping thus to secure, more speedily, means of support for his widowed mother and the younger members of the family. His partner in work was a well educated lawyer; and another of their party was a scientist who had been applying his knowledge of geology and mineralogy, in exploring; and had lately returned from a few miles south with a report so favorable they intended in a day or two to go and make a claim on his newly discovered ground. Here, then, was a party of California miners, dressed in the usual mining attire, and carrying pick, shovel and pans to and from their work; who yet were cultured gentlemen.

I soon found that this was by no means a solitary instance. But a much larger number of the miners belonged to other very valuable classes of society. Merchants, mechanics, farmers were all there in large numbers. So that in almost every mining camp there was enough of the element of order, to control, or very much influence, the opposite forces. These facts soon became apparent to me, and, ere long, I felt as secure in my tent with the curtain tied in front, as I had formerly felt with locked and bolted doors. There was, of course, the other element as elsewhere; but they themselves knew that it was safer for law and order to govern; and, with a few desperate exceptions, were willing, to let the lovers of order enjoy their rights and wield their influence. And the desperate exceptions were, for the time, so over-awed by the severe punishment some of their number had lately suffered, that, for a while, at least, in those early days, life and property were very safe in the mines; unless indeed you chose to associate with gamblers and desperados, in which case you of course constantly risked your money and your life. But, the same is true, in the heart of New York, Philadelphia, or London.

During my short residence, of only two months, in Weaverville I had but a few brief glimpses of the objectionable phases of society. Indeed, I ought not to say *glimpses*, for it was almost wholly through the ear, that anything of this kind came to me. There was on the opposite side of the ravine, some rods down, a large tent, or rather, two tents irregularly joined, which, at first, I heard called a boarding house, then found was a public stopping place for travelers; and afterwards it turned out to include a full fledged drinking and gambling saloon. From this place, at night, we sometimes heard the sound of loud talking; but I recollect only once hearing anything alarming from there. That was past midnight, one rainy, dark night, when we were startled from sleep by a loud shout, followed by various outcries, several running footsteps, and three or four pistol shots. We looked out and saw a light or two in the direction of the saloon but heard no more of the noise. The next morning we were told by one who had inquired, that a gambler who had lost several times, and saw himself about to lose again, had snatched all the money from the table by a sudden movement, and fled out into the darkness before any one had been aware of his intention. Then, two or three had followed with shots; but he had escaped them.

The other sound I caught from that direction, came

through a woman, the only one besides myself in the town. There had been another when I first came, a delicate, lovely invalid who, away back on the Platte River, had for awhile traveled in the same company with us, riding much on horseback in hope of benefiting her health. She and her husband stayed in Weaverville a short time but, when the rains began they sought the valleys farther to the south. This other woman who remained was a plain person who, with her husband, had come from one of the western states, and was acquainted only with country life. She was probably between thirty and thirty-five years of age, and the idea of "shining in society" had evidently never dawned upon her mind, when I first used to see her cooking by her out-door camp fire, not far from our tent. Ordinary neighborly intercourse had passed between us, but I had not seen her for some time, when she called one day and in quite an exultant mood told me the man who kept the boarding-house had offered her a hundred dollars a month to cook three meals a day for his boarders, that she was to do no dishwashing and was to have someone help her all the time she was cooking. She had been filling the place some days, and evidently felt that her prospect of making money was very enviable. Her husband, also, was highly pleased that his wife could earn so much. Again I saw nothing of her for some time, when again she called; this time much changed in style. Her hair was dressed in very youthful fashion; she wore a new gown with full trimmings, and seemed to feel in every way elevated. She came to tell me there was to be a ball at the public house in a few days; that several ladies who lived at different camps within a few miles, chiefly at Hang-Town, were coming; and she came to say that I might expect an invitation as they would like very much to have me come. I laughingly declined, as being no dancer, and entirely unfitted to adorn any such scene. The assembly I think came off, but I did not get even a glimpse of its glories; and as she, soon after, left the town, I never saw her again. I only remembered the circumstance because it amused me as being my first invitation into "Society" in California; and also as it gave me a glimpse of the ease with which the homeliest if not the oldest, might become a "belle" in those early days, if she only had the ambition; and was willing to accept the honor, in the offered way.

Soon after arriving in Weaverville, my husband had met with an acquaintance who had been a traveling companion in the early part of our long journey. He had washed out a little gold, and was desirous to go into business. He had made two or three acquaintances who also thought this new mining settlement presented an opening for a store; but none of them were accustomed to trading. They understood that my husband was; so they proposed to him to enter into partnership with them, proceed immediately to Sacramento City to purchase goods, and they, by the time he returned, would have a place prepared to open a store.

An effort was made to get a house built. The plan was, to hew out timber for the frame, and to split shakes for the roof and sides. But when they tried to get men to help them; so that the building could be done in anything like reasonable time, they found it impossible. All were so absorbed in washing out gold, or hunting for some to wash, that they could not think of doing anything else. On all sides the gold-pans were rattling, the cradles rocking, and the water splashing. So the best that could be done was, to hew out some strong tent poles and ridges, and erect two good sized tents, one behind the other; the back one for dwelling, the front for a store. An opportunity occurred to buy a large cook stove, which was placed near the junction of the two tents. The back part of the back tent was curtained off for me, leaving a space round the cook stove for kitchen and dining room. One of the men slept in the store, and the other two had a small tent on one side. They managed to buy some packing boxes, and other odds and ends of lumber, and so made shelves and a counter, which did very well for those primitive times.

We were soon fixed in our new quarters, the goods arrived from Sacramento, and business was opened. As one of the partners had formerly been in the meat business, some fat cattle were purchased, and beef was added to the other articles sold. This drew quite a crowd every morning; for fresh meat had not yet become very plentiful in the mines. It had not been thought necessary for all the men of the firm to devote their time to the store. Two of them continued mining; so, when a large number of customers came together, I helped to serve them. This gave me an opportunity to see most of the dwellers in Weaverville; and observe in a small way their behavior to each other. The majority of them were, as I have said, men of ordinary intelligence, evidently accustomed to life in an orderly community, where morality and religion bore sway. They very generally showed a consciousness of being somewhat the worse, for a long, rough journey, in which they had lived semi-barbarous lives, and for their continued separation from the amenities and refinements of home. Even in their intercourse with each other, they

[85]

often alluded to this feeling, and in the presence of a woman, then so unusual, most of them showed it in a very marked manner. But, mingled with these better sort of men who formed the majority, were others of a different class. Roughly-reared frontier-men almost as ignorant of civilized life as savages. Reckless bravados, carrying their characters in their faces and demeanor, even when under the restraints imposed by policy. All these and more were represented in the crowd who used to come for their meat, and other provisions in the early morning hours. There were even some Indians, who were washing out gold in the neighboring ravines, and who used to come with the others to buy provisions. It was a motley assembly and they kept two or three of us very busy; for payments were made almost exclusively in gold-dust and it took longer to weigh that, than it would have done to receive coin and give change. But coin was very rare in the mines at that time, so we had our little gold scales and weights, and I soon became quite expert in handling them. While thus busy, in near communication with all these characters, no rude word or impertinent behavior was ever offered me.

But, among this moving crowd, thus working and eating, buying and selling, sounds of discontent and sadness were often heard. Discontent; for most of them had come to California with the hope of becoming easily and rapidly rich; and so, when they had to toil for days before finding gold, and, when they found it, had to work hard in order to wash out their "ounce a day"; and then discovered that the necessaries of life were so scarce it took much of their proceeds to pay their way, they murmured; and some of them cursed the country, calling it a "God forsaken land," while a larger number bitterly condemned their own folly in having left comfortable homes and moderate business chances, for so many hardships and uncertainties. And still, many of them kept repeating this same folly, by being easily induced, when they had struck tolerably fair prospects, and were clearing twice as much per day as they had ever done before, to give up their present diggings, and rush off after some new discovery, which was sure to be heralded every few days, by the chronic "prospectors" who then, (as too commonly ever since) kept the whole community in a ferment.

But the sounds of sadness were deeper, and more distressing than those of mere discontent, for they were caused by sickness and death. Many ended their journey across the plains utterly prostrated by over-exertion, and too often poisoned by unwholesome food, and want of cleanliness. Three or four young men, living within a mile of us, had crossed the country from the Missouri to the mines in three or four months; and during that whole time, as they reported to their neighbors, they had not once taken off any of their clothing—not even their boots—and had lived on salt meat and "hardtack." Of course disease claimed them as natural prey. One of them died soon after arriving; the others suffered long; and, when we last heard of them, were still in a critical condition. But, aside from instances of glaring imprudence or ignorance, many felt the effects of long-continued over-exertion, extreme changes in temperature and ways of life, and, often, of sickening depression from the disappointment of too sanguine hopes. Those thus suffering were sad in voice and looks, needing all the cheering influence the healthy ones could afford. And many were the instances of brave, unselfish ministry among those often careless-appearing men. But, spite of kind efforts, and attentions, there were, in our neighborhood, two or three cases of death, and several of decided illness.

My husband came home from a trip to Sacramento, nearly prostrated by an attack of cholera-morbus, and was, for some days, disabled from ordinary duties. Just as he had nearly recovered, a slow but powerful fever laid me helpless for a number of days. As soon as I was able to be moved my bed was placed in a wagon, all the comforts and conveniences, that could very well be carried in that way, were put in with me, a seat was fixed for Mary close by my side and, on the 27th of December, just two months from the time we entered Weaverville we set out for Sacramento City.

By the date, it was nearly midwinter, but by the little tufts of grass on the road-side, it was the beginning of spring; and, as we descended the foot-hills, and struck the South Fork of the American River the season seemed to advance very rapidly. Flowers began to bloom in the turf, and early shrubs to blossom in the woods; while in the little thickets several species of birds flitted gayly about chirping and whistling their hints of the "good time coming." The genial atmosphere, bright sun and pleasant landscape assisted much in advancing my hitherto slow recovery. Appetite began to return, and, the second evening of our journey, when we camped near a house where entertainment for travelers was offered, I asked the landlady to bake for me a sweet potato, a luxury which had lately been introduced into the mines from "The Islands." She did so, and we paid seventy-five cents for it. They had no sleeping accommodations, that were as comfortable as my bed in the wagon, so we had no occasion to acquaint ourselves with their terms for lodgings. I have not thought it worth while to speak of prices in the mines, so much has been said on that subject in connection with every new mining settlement: but of course fresh meat was a half dollar per pound, butter a dollar, and other things in proportion. Yet we thought seventy-five cents for one baked sweet potato was quite equal to any charge we had heard of. However, when a few days afterward, in Sacramento City, one of our number paid a dollar for an onion, and another twenty-five cents for a quart of milk, and then saw the seller put water into the measure, we ceased to wonder at charges.

On the first day of January 1850 we arrived at Sutter's Fort; and I saw for the first time a spot of which I had heard and read away back in the Empire State, when, in laughing girlhood, I used to threaten I would go and see that Fort some day, and stand on the Pacific shore; though I hardly expected then to do so. We paused for an hour's nooning where I could see, from my seat in the wagon, the old buildings, surrounded by the wall whose wide gate now stood open. As I looked, and thought of all I had read about "New Helvetia," the certainty of being really on the once far off Pacific coast became stronger. We rode on, and, before evening closed in, were camped in the City of Sacramento.

[*In April, 1849, when Mrs. Royce had started across the plains, Sacramento City had consisted of four houses. By December the population was more than ten thousand.*]

There were more tents and cloth houses within sight than any other kinds of dwellings; and it was nothing strange to see a company living in a wagon; so we easily put up with that inconvenience for a day or two, till sufficient lumber was secured to lay a good floor, and over it was stretched a well made tent. In this our large cook-stove and several other newly-procured household conveniences were placed, and again we began house-keeping; though I was not yet able to sit up all day.

The intention was to build a house, as soon as possible, on this lot, which had been purchased before I came down, and here to open a general grocery and provision business. But the skies which had been so serene for a week or two, clouded over, the afternoon we got into our tent, and the great rain of the season set in. Day after day it kept on, with only short intervals of such lovely sunshine as we had never before seen in January. I, of course, could not go out a step to see anything, only stand at times in the doorway, when the sun broke out, looking at the soft green turf and the grandly broken clouds for a few minutes; then all would be shadow again, and rain, rain, rain would pour down for hours. Two of the partners in the mines had come with my husband, and were impatient to build and open business, but at present nothing could be done but attend to the cattle, part of the time every day. As they went and came I could hear, from my curtained corner, where in my weakness I had to spend much of my time, the news of the neighborhood and various discussions as to the probabilities of business, the weather, etc.

In a day or two they began to talk about the rise of the river, or, rather, the rivers, for both the Sacramento and American, I learned, began to look threatening; especially the latter, whose banks were very low just back of the City, where the old settlers said, it had more than once overflowed and filled "the sloo" sometimes spreading farther. Speculations about the danger were various; but, on the whole, the hope seemed to prevail that "the sloo" being lower than the ground where most of the city was located, would make a channel for the superfluous waters and let them flow away across the flats to mingle again with the Sacramento some miles below. So, though I knew there was danger, I did not dwell very anxiously upon it; but used every effort to recover strength.

On the evening of the 9th of January, I had put Mary quietly to bed and was resting myself for a minute or two before undressing for the night, when I heard quick footsteps without, and Mr. A——'s voice saying hastily to my husband who stood at the door, "The water's coming in." The reply expressed doubt; but A——'s voice continued very emphatically, "O, yes, I am sure, I have just been to the 'sloo,' and the water is flowing over the banks fast. See, come this way—to this low spot—and you will soon find yourself stepping in water. There, watch a minute—don't you see it rising on your boot?" A prompt assent was the reply, and I heard them in a few hasty words agree upon what was to be done. One of the few good houses within sight was the residence of a Dr. M—— and wife. He had come early to the country as an army surgeon, had quickly accumulated wealth, sent for his wife, and made a home in this fast growing city, where he owned several blocks of land. About a hundred yards from our tent he had lately built a story-and-a-half double house, intending it for rent in two tenements. It was not finished, but was inclosed and roofed, and two stairways were built one in each end of the house leading to the upper rooms. In the hurried words I heard between A—— and my husband, it was agreed that A—— should go to Dr. M——'s house and ask permission for us to take possession of one of those upper rooms; while my husband should prepare Mary and me for a hasty removal. While they were thus talking outside I had risen from my languid position, put on my rubbers and cloak, and had Mary in my arms dressing her when my husband came in. He saw that I had heard their conversation, and no explanations were necessary, so he went rapidly to work rolling up bed and bedding. I did what I could to help in gathering together, and putting into portable shape some of the conveniences most immediately needed, and which it was most essential to keep dry; and by the time A—— returned with permission for us to take possession of the desired room; we had several things ready to be removed.

Meantime, the water was filling up all the depressions, and, when we stepped out into the darkness, we soon found we must hasten, or it would be over shoe-tops. However, I managed with help to reach one of the front doors of the house, ascend the stairs and sit down on one of the bundles already there, with Mary safe beside me, ere the water had entirely covered the ground. Then sitting still there, I could hear the rippling and gurgling as it rose higher, and began to find its way into crevices and over sills in the lower story. It was evidently rising very fast. The men, kept coming and going between the tent and house, carrying such things as could be carried in the arms, and brought directly up stairs. But, even by the second time they returned, the water was up to their ankles, and it was not long before they were obliged to cease, and abandon to the flood all that remained.

[92]

By this time others had taken refuge in our little ark. A bed had been made in a corner, and blankets tacked up for a partition, and there Mary and I took refuge; while the men gathered round a stove that had been left there by some of the workmen who had boarded themselves while building. We could tell by the sounds through the partition-wall that a much larger number of persons had gathered in the other end of the house. Voices of all tones were heard there, from the stalwart bass to the shrill cry of infancy. We heard, the next day, that, by midnight, fifty persons had taken refuge in that part of the house, among them Mrs. Dr. M——— herself. Her home was on rather higher ground, and, though but one story in height, was for an hour or two, considered safe; but at last it became evident that the flood would soon cover the floors. Then, abandoning all but a few of the most necessary things, she was conveyed in a friendly boat to the little room where soon so many others had already flocked.

From the time we had found ourselves safe above the waters, the thought of the hundreds who must be exposed to the same dangers; and the wonder what could become of them, had been very distressing to me. But, as the first confusion subsided, and I found refuge in my curtained corner, I discovered, by the regular strokes of oars which every now and then passed near the house, and the voices mingled with them, that help was being very busily and efficiently rendered. I heard occasionally the words of some who came in boats and climbed into the windows of the house. Then, inquiries would be called out to others passing by, and answers given; by all of which I found that the boats of all the vessels lying in the river had been promptly manned and set in motion as soon as needed; that many other boats owned in the neighborhood were being freely used, and, that thus far, all who had been found in danger had been rescued. Hundreds had flocked, and were flocking to "the ridge," a strip of high land well above the water a mile or two east of where we were; many had been taken on board vessels in the river, and so, it seemed, thus far, all had been in some way provided for. This was very cheering, and as soon as the various voices, and other sounds became quiet, welcome sleep came to our relief.

In the morning boats were again heard close to the house, and I soon found out that most of those in the other part of the house were being conveyed away, either to go to San Francisco, or to the high ground back of the town. All, in our end, except our little party, also left, and as soon as I felt able, I managed to get dressed and go to the window. For miles north and south I could see nothing but water, bearing upon its surface boats, and various odd looking craft. Eastward the expanse of water was narrower, and, beyond it, was the ridge which looked much like an enormous Mississippi raft, covered with a dense mass of moving creatures of some kind, though it was impossible for the eye at our distance to distinguish them one from the other.

Soon some acquaintances of A—— and H—— came near in a boat and they let themselves down from the window into the little craft and went toward the ridge to see if they could get some fresh meat. They had previously been told by some passers-by, that provisions had been rescued from the stores the night before, and conveyed to the ridge in quantities sufficient to prevent a famine till more could come from San Francisco;

and fresh beef was being brought from the neighboring country. In due time they returned with such supplies, as, added to what had been saved the night before, secured us enough to live on for a few days. Sufficient stove wood had been hurried upstairs among the first things the night before, to cook several meals. Thus we were saved from danger of want for the present. The men had arranged with their friends who had boats to call at the window occasionally so that we might be sure of opportunities of communication with the "land beyond the flood," and also with the vessels on the river; for, already, the plan of going to San Francisco by the next steamer that could be taken, was under discussion. But for nearly a week there was no opportunity of getting down to the Bay, without such inconveniences and risks as seemed worse than our present position. There were at that time but two steamers running on the Sacramento, neither of them very fast, one, extremely slow. One had started down—the morning after the flood set in—so crowded with passengers and goods that there was neither safety nor comfort on board. The other was expected up in a day or two; but for some reason was delayed. Other vessels were taking passengers down, but were most of them too heavily loaded to be safe. So, for a number of days, Mary and I were absolutely imprisoned by the waters. The only outlook from our end of the house was toward the Ridge, and to the north and south. We could not look toward the river at all, and so had not the variety of seeing vessels arriving or departing.

As the men went and came they brought accounts by no means cheering of the condition of things on the Ridge. Many had escaped thither with very little to shield them from suffering or save them from want. Yet, those who had health, most of them managed to work bravely, and keep up hope. But there were sick ones there, poorly sheltered, and cared for but slightly. In two or three instances our men saw them dying, and heard them ask for friends to pray with them. In one or two places the dead lay stretched out ready for burial. But, worse still, the reckless and heartless were there; in some instances making the air ring with their discordant mirth, while they carried on their gambling and drinking.

There were accounts too, of some shameful instances of extortion which occurred the first night of the flood; in one of which it was said, a boatman refused to take on board a man who was clinging to the ridge of a small tent, almost submerged, until the latter should pay twenty dollars; which he declared he could not do, having lost all his money. The brutal fellow was about to row off, leaving the nearly drowned man to perish, when a heavily laden ship's boat came up. The Captain divined the difficulty at once, and under cover of a pistol compelled the first boatman to take aboard the suffering man, and row along-side the larger boat to a place of safety; assuring him that if he attempted to disobey orders he should be shot instantly. Such cases showed that there were about us desperately selfish men, who would stop at nothing for the sake of gain; but I am glad to say we heard of few such things; while instances of generous aid, and ready sympathy were common.

While we were thus water-bound, in a very ordinary, unfinished frame house—the water in the lower story reaching not far from half-way up to the rafters of our floor—there came a night of strong wind, rising, toward

midnight, to a heavy gale. Sweeping over so many miles
of water, it was not long in raising quite a sea. The
waves dashed against the sides of the house, shaking and
rocking it so that there seemed great danger of its
capsizing. The noise of wind and waves made sleep, for
some hours, impossible to me; and as I lay there in the
darkness I tried to prepare myself to seize Mary and
cling to whatever might be uppermost, in case the house
careened. But, through this danger, also we were merci-
fully preserved and, in a day or two afterward the old
steamer "McKim" was announced in port, and I was
told to be ready to depart on the morrow.

On the morning of the 15th of January a pretty good
sized boat was moored under the window; Mary was
handed down, and then, by means of a ladder firmly
steadied, I descended safely, and we were afloat. As we
neared the river-channel, we saw many more buildings
than were visible in our late neighborhood, and presently we were riding down the middle of a street with
houses on each side, some, dwellings only, then stores
with dwellings attached, then warehouses, one or two
hotels etc.; all submerged up to about half the height of
the first story. Most of them were, for the time, forsaken; though in some cases men were busy in boats,
fishing out various things from the ground floors, and
placing them up above; or carrying them away to safer
places. We had little difficulty in getting on board the
steamer, and, after some delay set off; but did not ar-
rive in San Francisco till the next morning.

Dreary were the sights on each side, as we steamed
slowly down the stream. For miles nothing but muddy
water, with here and there trees and shrubs, sometimes
singly, sometimes in clusters and groves, rising above

the surface. Occasionally there was a mound, or a ridge, reaching above the water; and, upon it, a group of cattle huddled shivering together. Shivering, not because the weather was cold, but because they were more or less wet, and had eaten but little for days. Sometimes there was a cabin or shanty on the rise, and one or two human forms could be seen. Once, and I think only once, a woman and a child or two, were seen with the men; and, very rarely, a stack of hay gave signs of forethought, and made one feel like shouting congratulations to the happy animals surrounding it. But that was a very unusual sight in those days, and has been too much so in the years since.

The morning of January 16th, 1850, we anchored in the Bay of San Francisco, at some distance from the shore. Directly in front of us was Telegraph Hill, and very cheery did it look to me, after all the dreary scenes of the past few days; with its sides, not then torn and disfigured as they are now, but clothed with bright verdure, and bathed in warm sunlight. The old, red building on its summit looked quaint and interesting with a bright-colored flag floating above it. It became an object of still greater interest, when I was told it stood there as a signal-bearer, keeping up communication between vessels outside the Golden Gate, and men in the heart of San Francisco.

It seemed that our steamer could not safely approach any nearer the shore; so the unloading of freight and passengers was effected by means of lighters. It was nearly noon when we landed on one of the wharves. I had to sit for awhile in a warehouse office, while my husband went to inquire for rooms, where we might put up. After some time he returned looking rather puzzled.

He said he had not been able to hear of a place where rooms, or even one room, could be got; but there was a public house not far off, where we could get dinner; and probably Mary and I could sit there for an hour or two, while he and Mr. A—— looked farther for rooms, or a house. Accordingly we walked, with not very elastic footsteps, to The Montgomery House, which Mr. A—— said they had been informed, was the best, if not the only hotel to be found within easy distance. It fronted on Montgomery Street not very far from Commercial. The building was long in proportion to its width, its frame work was frail, and was covered on the outside partly with boards, and partly with canvas, diversified, if I recollect rightly with sheets of zinc, in places that particularly needed staying, or had proved extra leaky. The inside was partly lined with cloth. The front door was in the middle of the gable end, and was reached by two or three rough board steps, from the decidedly muddy footpath which, then and there, was the sidewalk of Montgomery Street.

As we entered we were motioned to the right, where was a small room wholly without carpet, containing one table, and a very few chairs, and lighted by one window. This was the sitting room. The partition which separated it from the dining room behind it was of cloth. Across the little hall-way into which the front door opened, and directly opposite the sitting room door, was the bar room, a much larger apartment than the sitting room, and furnished with a box-stove, the only place for a fire in the whole house, excepting the cook stove in the kitchen; which latter apartment was behind the bar-room. From the little hall-way, and facing the front door ascended a flight of stairs. At the top of these you found yourself in a hall extending the whole length of the building, and of just sufficient width to allow a passage by the side of the stairway to the front end. The partitions on each side were wholly cloth, and, at distances of about four feet apart along the whole length of the hall, on both sides, were narrow doorways. Looking into one of these doorways, you saw before you a space about two and a half feet wide and six feet long, at the farther end of which was a shelf or stand, on which you could place a candlestick, while you had just room to stand and dress or undress. At the side of this space were two berths, one above the other; and these berths, so situated, were the only sleeping accommodations afforded by this hotel. Of course when I entered the house I had not the least idea of ever knowing anything about its sleeping accommodations. I supposed that in two or three hours, I should be in a private room, resting, preparatory to arranging a home nest. But when, after spending the afternoon searching, both the seekers returned and said nothing of the kind we wanted could be found; there was no alternative but to remain where we were.

The landlord thoughtfully proposed to the two lodgers who occupied the berths at the farther end of the hall, against the wall of the house, to give them up to us; thus placing us in the most private spot to be obtained; for which I certainly felt grateful. The next morning efforts to obtain a place to live were renewed, with similar results. An opportunity was offered of renting a whole house, which would be vacated in a few days, by a family going to the mines; but it was three times as large as we needed; besides being too lonely a place for me to be left alone in, while business was attended to.

Meantime, with all the discomforts of these surroundings, health was returning to me, and I was able to walk out a little with Mary. However, by turning to the right from the door, and going up a street which was then very steep, one soon got away from the water, and up to where there was a fine view of the Bay and the shores beyond. Up this hill I managed slowly to walk, and lead Mary, and very greatly did we both enjoy the warm sunshine, soft breeze and sparkling scene. Turning in a fresh direction, we came to where there were a number of odd looking shanties, several of them displaying in doors and windows strangely-shaped packages, many-colored boxes and, in some places, queer toys. It took me but a minute or two to see, that the people who stood in these doors, or walked busily about, were Chinese. I had seen but one or two since coming into San Francisco, and, before that, the only Chinese I had ever seen, was one who in my youth was brought by missionaries to America, and visited an Eastern city where I lived. This little nucleus of the since celebrated China-Town of San Francisco was to me, that January morning in 1850, an unexpected sight; and I was for a few minutes as much amused as Mary; but the out-landish look of every thing, soon made me feel out of place; and I was hastening to find a street I could turn down, when an elderly Chinaman with a long queue and blue cloth sack came from a store door, with smiling face, addressed to me a word or two in broken English, then stooped down, shook hands with Mary and placed in her hand a curious Chinese toy.

Now came a rainy day or two, greatly magnifying all

the disagreeable features of our surroundings. Everybody boarding at "our Hotel" was now obliged to keep within doors; and those not engaged in regular business had to spend the whole day, crowded into the little comfortless sitting room or huddled, as they could get chances, around the bar-room stove. There was necessarily much confusion; there were of course many there who were far from refined in manners; yet, I must say in all candor, that during those three very unpleasant days, I received no rough or discourteous word from anybody; I witnessed no offensive behavior; and, whatever there was of drinking at the bar, I saw no drunkards, either at the bar-room stove or in the sitting room. I was, repeatedly, very kindly invited to a warm seat at the stove with Mary; and never went there without finding room, cheerfully made.

But we could not live in this way long. Efforts were being made; but no place for us had yet been found. At last, on Saturday morning of this tedious week a new face appeared upon the scene, introduced by Mr. A——. It was the Rev. Mr. W—— Pastor of a Protestant Church, organized in San Francisco but a few months before. He had heard that a family were staying at the Montgomery House who wished to get rooms for housekeeping; and he came to give information and make a suggestion which he thought would be a relief. He said a friend of his had just built a house on purpose to rent in tenements. Only one tenement was yet finished and that one Mr. W—— was occupying with his small family; but another would soon be finished, which he thought we might get. Meantime, there was one room, besides his own apartments, which was habitable. We could no doubt secure that immediately, and

we could board in his family until a place was ready for
us to keep house. We were not long in availing ourselves
of this hospitable offer, and before night we were safely
sheltered, and our little comforts piled about us, in a
room which, though unfinished, was more comfortable
than any place we had occupied for many months.

⌊ The conveniences of civilized life, the comforts of
home, can not be keenly appreciated, or even fully seen,
by those who have never been, for a time, shut out from
them.⌉Repeatedly in the days that now followed, did I
find myself feeling that I had never before known the
brightness of the evening lamp-light, nor the cheeriness
of the morning breakfast room, with all their orderly
accompaniments; that I had never before realized the
worth of quiet domestic life, unworried by ever-threat-
ening dangers.

Still more impressive were the new emotions felt the
first time I attended Church in California. The building
was larger than I had expected; and I soon saw the
reason; for the numbers that gathered promptly, and
seated themselves, without hesitation, showed that a
large congregation was the ordinary rule. On each side
of the speaker's platform, which extended well forward,
the seats were arranged sidewise, and those nearest the
wall continued in that position for some distance; so
that, seated as I was near the center of the house, facing the pulpit, I had a nearly full view of a good many
faces. There were very few women; not more, I think,
than six or eight in the whole assembly. They were
dressed with the unassuming neatness common among
Christian ladies at the east, their manner was quiet,
self-possessed and devout, and they were treated by the
gentlemen with the courtesy always expected among

Americans, which of course, restrained every indication of marked notice. Yet, one could not help seeing, in most of the masculine faces, expressions of high appreciation and profound deference, as, by one's and two's, the few women entered and took their seats. A small choir occupied a low platform behind the congregation and, with their very good voices and correct time, led the plain familiar tunes; almost every one present joining heartily in the singing. Toward the close of the service a good anthem was well given by the choir. During prayer, quietness, reverence, devotion pervaded the assembly. When the speaker had announced his text and made one or two introductory remarks; the motionless quiet which prevailed drew my attention, and my eyes wandered to the mass of faces on each side the desk. Never before had I realized the sublimity of the human countenance. They were nearly all men, in youth, or in the prime of life. Every one was listening with fixed attention. There was an intensity of earnestness, a glow of intelligence in every face that made me involuntarily bow my head, and thank God for making so grand a being as man, and for letting me once more look upon so large a number, thus exercising the highest functions of intelligent beings, worshiping, adoring, and reverently receiving instruction from their Divine Creator. Whether the experiences through which those men had passed in the months just gone by, had taught them meanings in life, and power in spiritual truth they had never known before, thus illumining their faces, or whether I was favored that day in seeing an assemblage of exceptionally good men, I will not say; but such were my impressions of the first worshiping congregation I ever saw in California.

CHAPTER V
Morals

How swiftly, in that country, the Californians of the early days seized upon every suggestion that could give a sense of the unique importance of their new provincial life. . . . An entirely false interpretation of the doctrine of evolution has led some people to imagine that in any department of our lives, novelty as such must mean true progress toward the goal. . . . As a fact, what you and I really most need and desire is not the new, nor yet the old. It is the eternal. The genuine lover of truth is neither a conservative nor a radical. He is beyond that essentially trivial opposition. . . . Evolution itself is only a fashion in which the everlasting appears. For God there is nothing new. . . . Be ready to learn what is new to you. But avoid this disease of merely running after every thought that loudly proclaims, or every plan that stridently asserts, "Behold, I am new." Say to every such claimant for your reverences: "Are you such that you can grow old and still remain as good as ever? Then indeed I will trust you."

JOSIAH ROYCE, *Provincialism* and *On Certain Limitations of the Thoughtful Public in America.*

Morals

[*Josiah Royce in his* California *founded his discussion of the social life of San Francisco in the years immediately following the gold rush largely upon his mother's account of her observations. "The journey across the 'plains,'" he wrote, "and a few troubled months in the mines and at Sacramento, had led my father, after the great flood at the latter place, to come with my mother and her child to the Bay. . . . She passed a considerable time in 1850 in a little circle of San Francisco families that were held together mainly by those ties of social and religious sympathy that might be supposed to be most effective at such a moment, and in the midst of such exciting conditions." Mrs. Royce watched with sadness the disintegration of some of those families.*

The frontier was a tester of moral codes. To the new country of California came the codes of Mexico and of China. But the mass of the Californians had been trained with more or less success in the moral conventions which characterized the life of the settled East. Religion—Nineteenth-Century Puritanism—supported this code. Its adherents believed it to be the expression of the will of Absolute Authority. It was the embodiment of eternal truth, as changeless as the axioms of geometry. But on the frontier freedom reigned. In the new communities of California, swiftly forming and dissolving, the social sanctions of stable societies disappeared. In spite of Absolute Authority moral codes were transformed. The frontier, to the Puritan, was the stage for an elemental struggle between good and evil. Out of the conflict came new codes of morality.

Sarah Royce grieved to see men and women falter and fall when deprived on the frontier of the support of tradition. She knew that on every hand the forces of evil were winning victories. But she refused to admit the defeat of the good. She shared in the optimism of the age in America. She was an idealist. In spite of the decay of morals which she saw on every hand, she had faith that, in the end, the ideal would triumph.]

TWO months from the time we left the Montgomery House we began housekeeping in one of the tenements for which we had been waiting. The whole building was now completed, and being, for those early days, conveniently arranged and neatly finished, though with cloth and paper only, it was soon occupied by a number of the most respectable and companionable people in San Francisco. The owner himself established a boarding house in one part of it, and the other tenements were taken; in some cases by those who wished to board with him, in others by those who, like ourselves, kept house. Nearly all were from the eastern or the middle states, a very few were from the South. Most of them were church-going people. Some of them came to the house immediately on their first arrival in California, others had been in the city a number of months; but nearly all of them had some acquaintances in other parts of the town; and, as much sociability and kindly feelings prevailed, there was opportunity for the inmates of the house to get a fair insight into social life in San Francisco at that time.

Much has been said on this subject and many dark

pictures have been drawn. No doubt those dark pictures were true to life, in individual instances far too numerous; but just beside them, within the walls of neighboring dwellings, sometimes under the same roof, might have been drawn pictures, as true, of social circles in which refinement, morality and religion were as fondly cherished, and as faithfully illustrated in domestic life, as in homes on the Atlantic shore.

Any newcomer into San Francisco in those days had but to seek, in the right way, for good people, and he could find them. But in the immense crowds flocking hither from all parts of the world there were many of the worst classes, bent upon getting gold at all hazards, and if possible without work. These were constantly lying in wait, as tempters of the weak. A still greater number came with gold-getting for their ruling motive, yet intending to get it honestly, by labor or legitimate business. They did not at all intend, at first, to sacrifice their habits of morality, or their religious convictions. But many of them bore those habits, and held those convictions too lightly; and as they came to feel the force of unwonted excitement and the pressure of unexpected temptation, they too often yielded, little by little, till they found themselves standing upon a very low plane, side by side with those whose society they once would have avoided. It was very common to hear people who had started on this downward moral grade, deprecating the very acts they were committing, or the practices they were countenancing; and concluding their weak lament by saying "But *here* in California we *have* to do such things." Never was there a better opportunity for demonstrating the power and truth of Christian principle, than was, in those days, open to every faithful soul, and, never, perhaps, were there in modern, civilized, society more specious temptations to laxity of conduct. And thus it came to pass, that in this our early California life, while we had the pleasure of associating with those who were true to their convictions, earnest in their religious life, and faithful and lovely in the domestic circle, yet, on the other hand, we often met people, who had let loose the reins of moral government over themselves and families; and consented that others should do so.

A house constructed and occupied as was the one where we lived, which I have described, was a little world in itself; containing specimens of various types of character; and covering under its roof many phases of life. During the thirteen months we spent there, two little girls were born in the house into two different families; one death occurred of a man in the prime of life, for many years a sea captain; and one wedding was solemnized, and celebrated with considerable hilarity. Thus was completed within the small space the cycle of human events. But we who dwelt there were connected with many others outside, and so were in contact with the life in general of the city and the state.

We saw the beginnings of that system of "street grading" which has since so transformed the face of the site of San Francisco. We gazed with terror on the awful fire of May 4th, 1850. We witnessed the erection of new churches, and the inauguration of religious newspapers. As the year advanced we experienced the alarm of approaching cholera. We lived through the days when it paced slowly hither and thither in the city, striking down one here and another there, but never raging as an epidemic; while, at the same time, we were hearing daily of its fearful ravages in Sacramento City, the only place in California where it has ever prevailed alarmingly and, that year the only time.

In the early fall of 1850 we were all excitement to hear the result of California's knock at the door of the Union; and as the day approached when the steamer would bring the decision, many eyes were strained toward Telegraph Hill. At length the signal went up— the Oregon was outside the heads and would soon be in the harbor. As she neared, another signal indicated that she carried flying colors, implying good news, and presently she appeared in sight of those, who like ourselves overlooked North Beach, gay with streamers and flags of all nations,—the Stars and Stripes most prominent, and, above them, straightened out by the generous wind which seemed to blow a long breath on purpose, floated the longest streamer of all, displaying the words "California Admitted"! The roar of cannon rolled over the waters, and met answering roars from fort and ships. Everybody was laughing. "Now we were at home again!" cried one. "Yes," was the answer, "and remember, all, we must no more talk of going to 'The States' nor hearing from 'The States.' We are *in* 'The States'!" Well do I remember the brisk tap at my door that morning, and the friendly voice that invited me up to a high veranda to take a look, through a large field glass, at the welcome steam-ship. For some minutes we stood there looking in silence—the sight brought thoughts too many and too absorbing for words. Then, with brief expressions of thanksgiving and mutual congratulations, we descended, meeting and answering, as we passed through the halls and porches, the laughing congratulations of our fellow-inmates. This was in October of 1850.

But during the spring and summer of that year, the business marts of San Francisco were the scenes of speculations, of venturesome investments, of reverses and successes, which, to record, would take volumes; and the effects of which still live, for good or ill, in the lives of hundreds of Californians. It is sometimes said that all the old Pioneers are poor men. Doubtless this is too sweeping. Quite a number of those Pioneers laid the foundation, even in those early days of extravagant undertakings, for permanent business, and substantial prosperity. With clear heads, steady nerves and conscientious principles, they persevered in whatever line of business they had undertaken, and thus secured for themselves, in some cases great wealth, in more, a competence, and are now among the pillars of Californian society, with well educated families grown up about them, who, in their turn, are rearing children to follow in the good paths of their grand-sires. But the temptations to rash speculation were, in those days, very great; and there were men who came here from broken-down enterprises in the East, chafed nearly to desperation and, determined to make almost any venture to recover themselves. Others came comparatively inexperienced, but with inflated ideas of their own business capacities, and of the opportunities this new business world would surely open to them. Here and there, was an individual in whom all the conditions just named, met, and that man was bound to make a desperate dash, and as certainly bound to fail, and, alas, almost as certainly, bound to repeat the same experience every three or five years since, till, "The old Californian *is* a poor man."

But nothing could arrest or neutralize the natural results of reckless speculation, extravagant expansion, and bad management. It was not alone in the cities, and in ordinary commerce that these wild things were done. Men entered into contracts to buy herds of cattle, intending to turn them into beef, to supply the San Francisco market; and found on starting into the enterprize that catching the cattle, and getting them to where they could be handled, required more men and horses than they could get; besides involving other enormous expenses, which they had not taken into account. In other cases large tracts of land were purchased with the intention of making them cattle ranges or of cutting hay; but the purchase being chiefly on credit, or with borrowed money, and the returns being long in coming, interest ate up the purchaser, and often involved him hopelessly. In the mines, it soon became an admitted adage that "mining was a lottery"; but it was not more so, than such business enterprises as these.

In the social life of San Francisco, one of the sensations of that year, was an entertainment, got up for the benefit of a Benevolent Society which, even in that early day, had been organized months before, and had done, and continued doing, works of mercy, which cheered and saved many a lonely wanderer. The entertainment was conducted by the ladies of the different churches, of which there were, in the city, already four. Every thing went prosperously on the day of the festival, and in the evening a large crowd gathered for social enjoyment. Introductions, and cordial greetings were turning strangers into friends, and making many,

hitherto lonely, hearts feel, that even in California there
was society worth having, when there entered the room
a man, prominent for wealth and business-power, bearing upon his arm a splendidly dressed woman, well
known in the city as the disreputable companion of her
wealthy escort. With cool assurance he proceeded to
make her and himself quite at home; but in a few minutes he was waited upon by a committee of gentlemen,
who called him aside, and told him they were sent, by
the lady-managers to say that they declined to receive
as an associate, or to have introduced to their daughters, one who stood in the relation occupied by his companion, and they respectfully requested him to invite
her to withdraw with him. Of course there was nothing
for him to do but to comply; and all went on again
pleasantly. It was reported that he had previously
boasted that he could introduce "Irene" any where in
San Francisco, but the events of that evening proved to
him, as well as to others, that while Christian women
would forego ease and endure much labor, in order to
benefit any who suffered, they would not welcome into
friendly association any who trampled upon institu-
tions which lie at the foundation of morality and
civilization.

But, while this lofty and decided stand was taken
upon these important points by the wise; and was ap-
proved even by the less judicious, there were some
habits gaining ground among the thoughtless and selfish
which gave me uneasiness; and which I could not help
feeling presaged evil for the future. One of these was
the custom, early begun, of gentlemen manifesting their
gallantry by expensive presents to their lady acquaintances. This seemed to be done at first in a sort of off-

handed, jocular way; probably without much thought
as to its motives or results. There were but few ladies.
It was natural there should be a little feeling of rivalry
among the gentlemen in competing for the favor of
those few. Money, while it was easily lost, was in those
days, often as easily won. When a gentleman of social
disposition "made a strike," as they commonly expressed it, he often liked to tell his lady friends in a
laughing way of his good management or unexpected
luck. An easy way to introduce the subject was jokingly
to toss at her, or in some way offer, a pretty present;
and tell her it was a treat on the strength of "so and
so."

There were, I am glad to say, ladies of such dignity
of character and self-respect as to prevent, without direct effort, any such advances; but there were too many
whose cupidity and vanity were stronger than delicacy
of feeling, or sense of propriety; and I blushed to dis-
cover, by conversations held in my presence, that there
were instances of women watching each other, jealously,
each afraid the other would get more or richer presents
than herself. This evil became painfully prominent, as
time went on and more families came to the coast, in
connection with musical and literary entertainments,
school exhibitions, etc. Little girls and young ladies who
sung, played, or recited on such occasions often received, thrown at their feet before they left the stage,
expensive jewelry, or even pieces of coin. They commonly accepted them; often with looks of exultation;
and, still worse, there were mothers, who not merely
countenanced the thing, but even boasted of the amount
their daughters had thus received. It must indeed be an
obtuse moral sense that could not perceive the corrupt-

ing tendency of such customs; and I have since seen some sad falls into positive vice of those whose downward course appeared to begin in these and similar practices.

For nearly three years after our first arrival in San Francisco, we lived on the borders of the Bay. Less than half the time was spent in the City, the remainder, nearly all, in one of the most beautifully located villages, that the steamboat traveler of those early days admired, as he journied from the metropolis to the interior. During those two or three years there first came under my observation some of the unfavorable effects of the great California emigration movement upon American domestic life. The first case which called my attention to the subject, was that of an acquaintance whom we had met on the plains, and who had ever since continued, at short intervals, to turn up somewhere in our vicinity, wherever it might be. He had from the beginning of our acquaintance been very free in telling about his wife and family; in a . . . way which gave the impression at once that he and they belonged to that ordinary, matter-of-fact class, among whom we were accustomed to see the domestic relations so naturally stand intact, that the idea of the breaking up of such a family by anything but death, never used to occur to us. I was therefore much surprised, on being told by him, that he had received intimations from a friend in Illinois to the effect that his wife was likely to seek a divorce from him. He for awhile appeared to feel deeply pained and mortified by the position of things; but, as time passed, he seemed to care less; and when, after a number of months, he announced that she had done as was predicted, there were no signs of a broken heart.

Indeed after hearing the man talk on the subject several times, and seeing the light in which he viewed things, I came to doubt much whether California was in any way responsible for the event. Shallow, weak natures in whom selfishness predominates do not furnish depth of soil for the growth of life-long affection, or of the patient endurance that is faithful to sacred ties, even when suffering from coldness and neglect. But then, California had furnished the occasion of this estrangement and final separation; so of course California was blamed for it, as also, for various other similar events.

Hints were sometimes heard in conversation, and occasionally appeared in newspaper paragraphs, to the effect that single men were proving a dangerous element in society, by insinuating themselves into the affections of married women, and, in some cases, supplanting husbands. I saw no instance of this kind myself until several years later.

But, in the domestic life of those early days, it was not always the husband that was neglectful and indifferent nor the wife that was faithful. I knew a woman whose every need was richly supplied, her every wish kindly considered by her husband, and, whenever within his means, gratified. He built, as soon as his business allowed, one of the best dwellings to be found in the city where they lived. All was planned according to her directions, and modified to suit her whims. Yet, she was never contented. Pleasant words and smiles rarely greeted him. Imperious demands, and cold criticism embittered his life. He bore it patiently, and meant to keep on enduring; for the sake of those sacred laws to which he ever acknowledged unswerving allegiance. But she contrived in some way, I never knew how, to get possession of a large portion of his property; and then to obtain a divorce. There must have been sad corruption somewhere, or she could never have carried it through.

Another instance of a woman's unfaithfulness, came painfully under my notice. Her three children were, for some time, my pupils; the oldest, a girl just entering her teens, was rather remarkable for her good sense and womanly stability. The mother must have married early, for she was still young and quite handsome. The father was a man of good sense, average intelligence, and manners by no means disagreeable. Their home, whenever I saw it, seemed well furnished with comforts. But the fatal gift of beauty which the mother possessed, accompanied as it was by a weak vanity, laid her open to the flattery of the designing; and within two years of the time when I first knew them, the saddened father was left with no one but his thirteen-year-old girl to manage his forlorn household.

Then there was Mrs. D———. How beautiful she was; so beautiful that when I first saw her it was difficult to remove my eyes from her face. If it had only been a picture on which I could look long without offence. But then, it was the life that made the chief charm; and I could not wonder at the evident admiration with which a remarkably fascinating neighbor of ours regarded her. But when that neighbor became more and more frequently her companion in her walks, as she passed by our retired nook, I sighed, not only for her sake and her husband's but for their three little girls. The end came rather slowly; but it came at last. She herself in the paroxysms of a terrible illness, told her husband of her own fall and of her repugnance to him; and he, with shame and pain, took those three little girls to his mother and sisters in the far East, never to see *their* mother again. How can she bear to look back to their baby-hood? How can she endure to think of the work *she* has wrought into the fabric of California social life?

CHAPTER VI

Fortitude

But, after all, fidelity and family devotion are amongst the most precious opportunities and instances of loyalty . . . the only possible ethical use of an individual is to be loyal. He has no other destiny.

JOSIAH ROYCE, *The Philosophy of Loyalty.*

Fortitude

BUT it is a relief to turn from these sad pictures, to the memory of that flowery spring, in the beginning of which I first entered, what I then believed to be, the most lovely village in California. Every smoothly-rolling hill was dressed in bloom; and the flat land of the valley stretched like a gorgeous carpet from the center of the village far back toward the foot of a grand old mountain. The air was full of the songs of answering meadow-larks, occasionally enriched by a glee from the more retiring mocking-bird. It was virtually my first California spring; for the only one I had previously seen in the state, was spent in San Francisco, where, while I saw and enjoyed the softly-smiling skies; the brilliant sunshine, the calmly-sleeping waters of the Bay, and the rolling hills beyond, still I could not be out among the grass and flowers: all I saw of spring was in the distance; and very soon the summer winds and fogs, peculiar to San Francisco, ended the season for much out of doors enjoyment. But in our pretty village, or rather just on its outskirts, as I was, I had only to open the doors, and grass, and flowers, and birds, were all about me.

Then, the children enjoyed it so much. The older one ran about, picking flowers and making play-houses, while the baby sat in her cradle, or her little chair, near the door, crowing and laughing, and watching the other. Life can never be very lonely or dull to a mother who sees her children healthful and happy, and who has

[123]

faith in the constant presence of the great and good One, her own Helper and Friend, and the Guardian of those little treasures for whom she gladly cares and toils.

Our pleasant village at that early day could scarcely be expected to own a church building, but there was a school house, and in it were held meetings, most of the time, on every alternate Sunday. The preaching was usually by Methodist ministers, coming either from a neighboring town, or from San Francisco. Sometimes a clergyman of the Cumberland Presbyterian denomination officiated. There was usually a fair congregation for the size of the place; and it is needless to say that those composing it were among the most intelligent and respectable people of the town. We had a little Sunday School; and considerable interest was shown in it by the ministers; as well as by some of the best educated people of the neighborhood. There was no formal church-organization; as the members of the congregation and the workers in the Sunday School belonged to three or four different denominations. But, as they agreed on the great foundation facts and principles of Christianity, harmony seemed to prevail among them.

As the season advanced, surrounding colors changed. The green of the hills became flecked with faded spots, which gradually spread, till nearly the whole surface was of a rich old-gold . . . and the wild oats stood in their proud maturity, boasting their wealth. But when the breeze swept over them, they had to bow, and dance, and laugh in merry sparkles; while the ever-green oaks, which here and there waved their boughs slowly above them, seemed conscious of the superior dignity of their richly-dark robes. Wild flowers still added, here and

[124]

there, a dash of color, and the pasturing herds, moving, or at rest, gave life to the scene.

One hot August afternoon when I was, as usual, alone with the children, as I passed across our kitchen-dining-room, near the open front door, my eye was caught by a moving object on the ground outside, coming toward the house, I stopped to look. It was a creature covering a space which looked to me about the size of an eight year old boy's hand. In the center was a round, hairy body terminated by a projecting hairy head, while legs looking like slender, hairy fingers, with the knuckles well set up, strode on each side making fast time towards the house. I had never seen one before, but I had read of them, and knew it in an instant. It was a tarantula! The first thought was that it would get under the house. Then I could not find it. It might crawl through some opening up into the house; when and where I shuddered to think, as Mary's low bed, and baby's cradle, came into my mind. It might get to where the children were then playing not far from the house. These thoughts all flashed through me in an instant, and at the same time I sprang out of the back door, seized a short heavy chunk of wood, ran round the end of the house so as to intercept the creature's path, and dropped the weapon directly upon it.

I had literally crushed the enemy; but I could not for some time get over a constant impulse to scan closely the whole premises, and peer into every corner and aperture. However, I never saw another tarantula near the house: and a friend to whom I showed the remains and who had been familiar with the creatures, both here and in Mexico, said it was unusual for them to be seen except in very undisturbed places. He also assured me that it was, really a decidedly large specimen; and I got credit for having conquered a formidable foe; for, he said, if I had struck it with a stick and not at once disabled it, it would most likely have sprung at me. He had seen Mexican boys tease them in this way before killing them; and the boys had to be quick in their motions to escape being bitten.

The season rolled on, and brought the kindly, springlike winter, with just enough of rain and storm to water well the earth, brighten the whole landscape, and make the sunny intervals seem like days come out of Paradise. Then another spring spread its verdant mantle, strewed its gorgeous flowers, scattered their fragrance into our faces till we were almost intoxicated with delight, won us out to walk and ride among its beauties, then made way for another rich, luxurious summer, which in its turn faded into a pensive autumn, whose air seemed full of mournful yet tender prophecies, and still I lived in that same little village. As I look back to the months I spent there, it always seems to me that there was then granted to me an extra installment of youth; so unexpectedly rich and fresh were the experiences that came to me during that time. Not that I was rich in worldly goods, nor in surroundings that are ordinarily supposed to make life happy. But there are spiritual treasures; experiences of heart and mind, the joy of having done good to some struggling soul, the gladness of witnessing and sharing victory over evil, the certainty of a Guiding Presence, always near; these things bring a delight to the spirit which never comes from mere outward prosperity.

About the middle of that fall I again journied toward the interior of the State. But by this time the face of

things was much changed. We went to live in a little
mining town, not in the mountains as before but on a
river, within about twenty miles of Sacramento City.

[*When Mrs. Royce returned to the mining country,
the long and bitter struggle for law and order had been
won. In the first years of statehood each town had been
almost an independent community where turbulence and
vice were but slightly restrained. "In the mines," wrote
Royce in his* California, *"naked fortune was a more
prominent agent than in the cities or on the coast.
Plainly the first business of a new placer community
was not to save itself socially, since only fortune could
detain for even a week its roving members, but to get
gold in the most peaceful and rapid way possible. Yet
this general absolution from social duties could not be
considered as continuing indefinitely. The time must
come when, if the nature of the place permitted steady
work, men must prepare to dwell together in numbers,
and for a long period. Then began the genuine social
problems. Everyone who came without a family, as a
fortune-hunter whose social interests were elsewhere,
felt a selfish interest here in shirking serious obliga-
tions; and among such men everybody hoped, for his
own person, soon to escape from the place. And yet, if
this social laziness remained general, the effect was simply inevitable. . . . The social sins avenged themselves,
the little community rotted until its rottenness could no
longer be endured; and the struggle for order began in
earnest, and ended with the triumph of order, and the
securing of permanent peace, or else only when fortune
sent all the inhabitants elsewhere."*

*The culture level of the mining country to which
Mrs. Royce was returning is adequately described in*

[127]

the names given to the camps—Poker Flat, Gomorrah,
Ground Hog Glory, Hell-out-for-Noon City, Slumgul-
lion, and Delirium Tremens.]

The sands of the river-bed were said to be rich in
gold, which, of course, could only be washed out while
the bed was dry, in the summer. But, besides this, gold
had been discovered in the bluffs and banks on the north
side of the stream, and for washing this out, a large
supply of water was needed. A number of San Francisco
gentlemen had organized themselves into a company to
meet this want. Their plan was, to dam the river some
distance above the bar, raise the water, by means of a
steam engine, to the required height, run it through a
large flume, back of the diggings, and enough above
them to give a sufficient fall, then sell the water to the
miners, by the square inch, distributing it by means of
small flumes as it was required. The necessary buildings
were erected, the steam engine constructed, the great
flume built, the whole involving an enormous expense;
and while this was being done there was a gathering of
miners—among them a very few families. Tents and
cloth houses were put up, occasionally a shanty, half
logs and half boards, and one or two very inferior
board houses. We located ourselves upon a very pretty
spot on the bluff, within the shadow, of two or three
thrifty young oaks, and having on each side of us clusters of clean shrubbery, almost as pretty as a cultivated
hedge, making for us, a kind of enclosure.

Our house was of cloth; but the frame of it was excellent; as was proved, within a few weeks after we entered it, by one of the longest and most terrific gales I
ever experienced in California, accompanied by very
heavy rain. For three days and nights did the floods

descend and the winds beat. Our timbers bent, till the whole frail tenement seemed stooping under the strain; but, by a kind Providence, it weathered the blast; and, though there was some leakage in two or three places, we were on the whole tolerably comfortable, and the thing which I most dreaded—bad colds for the children —did not occur.

Our house was not very large; but I contrived to make-believe quite an imposing establishment. In the first place I covered the floor entirely; partly with matting, partly with dark carpeting. One end I curtained off for a bedroom, and by having a trundle bed for the two older children, (I had three now) I managed to make room for hanging up clothing, and for standing trunks. The rest of the house I divided—more by the arrangement of the furniture than by actual partition —into kitchen, dining room, and parlor. The cookstove, wood-box, and a cupboard, which I made with my own hands from a dry-goods box, about covered the space that I could conscientiously call kitchen. My dining room was not much larger; and was furnished with a table and a couple of chairs; and if I did have to use my dining table in preparing my bread, pies and cakes on baking days, I did not have very far to go to put them into the oven, nor much farther, to put them in the cupboard, when done and cooled.

But the parlor—that was my pride. There was against the wall, a small table, covered with a cloth, and holding a knick-knack or two, and a few choice books. Above it was a narrow shelf with some other books, and some papers. There were two or three plush-covered seats, which Mary and I called "ottomans." Their frames were rough boxes, which I had stuffed and covered myself. The rocking chair, when not required near the stove for baby, was always set in the parlor beside the table, suggesting leisure and ease: but the pride of all, was my melodeon. It was said to be the first one that was ever brought to California. It came round the Horn, had been used for a year or two in a church in Sacramento; and now was, by unusual good fortune, mine. One of the "ottomans" answered for a music-stool. There was little time for music during the day, except on Sundays; but at night when, the children were all in bed and the store—for we had a store again—kept my husband away, I used often to indulge myself in the melodies and harmonies that brought to me the most precious memories of earth, and opened up visions of heaven. And then those bare rafters, and cloth walls became for the time a banquet-hall, a cathedral.

But our life in this locality was short, for it turned out in a few months, that the expenses of the Water Company were so great, they could not let the miners have water without charging so high as to take nearly all that could be made by mining. They had meetings, and tried to make compromises, but the San Francisco capitalists showed that the enormous sums they had invested, and the necessary expenses of running the engine, made it impossible for them to furnish water at the rates the miners required; while the miners demonstrated as clearly that to pay for water at the Company's rates was ruinous to them. So, after two or three meetings, in which some rather stormy and many quite pathetic speeches were made, depicting the sad disappointments of the great men who had built the great works, the parties parted. The next morning there appeared in monstrous, white, chalked letters, on the side of the big flume, the words, "Dried Up." . . . Soon, tents were struck, houses taken down, store broken up, and the once busy mining "Bar" was almost deserted. We heard afterward that wiser heads planned and executed the simple contrivance, of a ditch tapping the river several miles above, and so conducting water by its own natural force, instead of expensive machinery, through a large area of moderately rich surface diggings. In this way a great deal of profitable mining was done for years afterward, on this very ground where the great failure occurred.

Early in the morning of a very hot day in early summer, our little family were once more seated in a well packed wagon—to be followed by another one—and the horses heads were turned toward the Sierras. Not that we intended to ascend the mountains. Our destination was another mining camp, some miles up, in the foot hills. The intention was to seek a favorable spot near the camp, which was a very flourishing town, settle upon the ground, claim it as a homestead, and make a family residence of it; while business might be carried on in the town.

A pretty spot within a mile of the camp had been decided upon previous to our removal, as a good place to pitch our tent, and there we stopped at the end of that hot day. When, the next morning, we examined our surroundings every thing looked so favorable it was decided to remain, while farther investigation was made as to the opening for business in the village. This latter prospect was found good; but it soon turned out that the place where we were staying was already claimed by a party who had begun improvements a little distance off. So, after a few days of prospecting, it was determined to make a claim farther from the mining town, on the main road from Sacramento to the mountains. Accordingly a man or two set to work and reared our cloth house, which had been brought, with the frame, from our late place of abode.

It was put up in a little grove of quite young, and rather slender oak trees, which when the sun shone threw their shadows on the white, transparent walls so distinctly that when inside, with the door shut, one could almost trace out the leaves on the canvas. A few feet from the house, on one side, was a group of bushes, growing in such a way as to form almost a semicircle; while two or three young oaks, growing among them threw a grateful shade over the almost inclosed spot. With a bit of awning stretched over the least sheltered side, and a few yards of cloth tacked from one tree to another on the side toward the road, a delightful kitchen was at once improvised. Here our cook-stove was set up, our cupboard placed on a box to raise it from the ground, then fastened firmly to a tree, our dining table and a few seats arranged at a little distance, and, at once, we had not only kitchen, but dining-room; pleasanter, for the season and situation, than in-door rooms could be. This gave me the whole inside of my house for bed-room and parlor, so that my establishment was now quite aristocratic. When I had once more spread my carpeting and arranged my furniture, I sat down to my melodeon and made the woods and the pretty little hills ring with some of my favorite songs: while the two older children, delighted with their new surroundings decked a play-house with acorns and wild flowers; and baby, in the large square box I had carpeted and lined for her, alternately peeped over its sides at them and me, or pulled herself up by her little fingers, which could nicely reach its edge, and crowed with delight at this newly found power. Our house was several rods back from the road, and so out of the dust, while, being on a gentle elevation, we had a full view of all passers-by, whether riding or walking. It was a beautiful spot but lonely; for the nearest house one way was a half mile, in the other direction, still farther.

The new arrangement in business caused me to be left much alone with the children. In the bright sunny days, while they played about me, and I was busied with household cares, or sewing, I never felt lonely, at least not in a dreary way, and, even in the evening reading or writing would so occupy my mind as to keep me from timid apprehensions. But when, by and by, journeys to Sacramento, or up into the mountains caused me to be sometimes left alone all night, it did seem a little dangerous. There were a few Indians in the vicinity, two or three of whom had once or twice straggled by, and paused to gaze, with some curiosity. But they were not formidable, and I would not allow myself to care much about them.

When however, one hot afternoon, two men came from the road for a drink of water, one of them an English sailor, not prepossessing in appearance, the other a foreigner—who the English man said came from Malacca—having one of the most ferociously savage-looking faces I ever saw; I did become decidedly nervous. They took their drink and did not stay long; but I could not keep that horrid face out of my mind long together, and every time I thought of it, a sense of the utter defenselessness of my position would force itself upon me. I knew I was to be alone that night, and as

evening approached, I grew more and more wary and
sensitive to every sound; till by the time the children
were in bed and asleep I felt as if I should never be
sleepy again. I had, before dusk, made everything as
snug as possible in our outdoor apartment and now,
putting out my light, that it might not attract notice I
prepared to act as watchman for the night.

I had made, for the hot weather, two windows in our
house. This was done by ripping, in the vertical seams
of the cloth wall, a space of about eighteen or twenty
inches in length, then rolling back the two edges away
from each other, right and left and pinning them midway of the open space, so making a diamond shaped
window. One of the windows was by the side of the front
door, the other looked out toward the kitchen. Whenever I wished to close them I took out the pins, when
the edges pulled themselves together, and the canvas
being elastic enough for me to lap them a little, I
could, by using pins sufficient, make them nearly as secure as if sewed. On this night of my lonely watch, I
let the edges fall together, that no dark space might be
seen from outside, then took my station at the window
beside the front door. By placing a finger or two in the
bottom of the slit I could plainly see the whole space
between the trees from the house to the road.

It was bright moonlight and all looked so beautiful
and peaceful that I felt soothed, and pleasant, sacred
thoughts relieved my anxiety; but I did not feel at all
sleepy. I hummed, very softly, some sweet verses, to
dear old tunes; and precious companionship seemed to
gather about me. I was losing all sense of fear when a
shrill, loud, long bark, ending in a prolonged howl,
startled me. It was in the direction of the kitchen, and

I went softly to the slit on that side, and peeped out. After a few moments of entire silence, there was a rustling in the bushes beyond the stove, and soon there appeared out of the shadows a full sized coyote. He walked all about our little enclosure, smelt at every box and bag, tried with his nose to open the cupboard and seemed for some time bent on depredation: but failing in finding anything to suit him, by and by he trotted off into the woods again.

I returned to my seat at the front slit, again all alive to the least sound that might stir the air. After some time there was a little movement, at first so slight it might be just a faint breeze rising; but no, not a leaf stirred. The sound became regular—it was a footstep —it was approaching along the road from the direction those men had taken. Was there more than one? I could not tell—they might be keeping step together. The sound came nearer. In a moment I should see somebody come in sight. The step ceased—then the form of a man moved cautiously out from the shadow of the bushes, and turned from the road towards the house. I scarcely breathed. In a few paces he stopped, stood perfectly motionless, and evidently listened; then turned toward the road again. Was he going to call his companion? No, he tended the other way; he reached the road, then walked directly on, passing straight by and I heard his step keeping regular time till quite out of hearing.

The tension of my nerves had been so great, the re-action was inexpressible. Still I kept my watch; but all remained quiet. As that danger had passed so harmlessly why might I not relax my guard? It was getting towards morning—I would rest. So I lay down and slept till the sun was shining full on the front of the house. I dressed, and was nearly ready to go to my kitchen and prepare breakfast, when a quick step was heard coming up the path from the road, straight to the house, and directly there was a tap on the frame work of the door. I said, "Who's there?" and a laughing voice answered—giving the name of an old friend who once, for a while, was an inmate in our family when we lived down at the Bay.

We were soon chatting sociably in the kitchen, and having breakfast with the children; while we enjoyed a hearty laugh, as it came out in conversation that it was he who had caused my almost breathless fear of the night before. He had, the day before, come by stage from Sacramento to a town six or seven miles from our place and, determining to visit us, had made some inquiries about the road; and started to walk it rather late in the day. It turned out to be farther than he had supposed; so that when he found himself in front of the house he knew it must be fully ten o'clock. He paused, and then walked a little towards the house thinking he might hear us talking; but finding all still he determined to go on to the public house, which, having some previous knowledge of the neighborhood, he knew was about a half mile distant. . . . In two or three hours my husband came home, and for a few days I had plenty of company and protection. I played and sung old favorite pieces, we talked and walked, and, one day ascended a high hill which I had often noticed with interest, as it was the only thing within sight of the house that looked like a mountain. But, in a few days I was alone again—and I felt it worse than ever. One of my lonely nights soon after that, brought a little bright incident, which I always like to recall. I had awakened in the middle of the night, which was very dark, to attend to some want of one of the children, and was just ready to lie down again when suddenly all was light as day. The branches and leaves of the trees threw their shadows on the canvas as in sunlight. I had time to think, "It is a fire! no, it is too white a light for that, it is a meteor!" when all was dark again. A day or two after when my husband came home, the papers he brought gave accounts of a remarkable meteor which was seen that very night passing over Sacramento and some of the foothill towns. . . .

Another dark night brought a less agreeable sensation. From a very sound sleep I was awakened by the tramp of horses, and at the same moment heard a man's voice, close by, say distinctly, "I know she's alone, for I saw her husband going away this morning and he said he would be gone two days." A creeping chill came over me. Another voice, lower and less distinct, replied. Then my name was called very emphatically. I answered as firmly as I could, and in what I meant should be a defiant tone. The first voice then said, "We didn't want to frighten you, but we are looking for a lost man, and we called to ask if you have heard anybody making any noise about here." I said "no" and asked further explanation. It seemed that two of the men at the neighboring public house, had ridden, the preceding day, to town, and started for home in the evening. One of them had been drinking a good deal, and was restive about leaving town, urging the other to turn back with him. The other became tired of his obstinacy and rode off, thinking his companion would follow when he found his entreaties vain. Late at night the horse of the drunken man came home without the rider; and the men who had so startled me were out hunting for him. They passed on; but I did not soon go to sleep again. In about an hour I again heard horses' feet, and a voice called out in passing, "We've found him; he was lying by the road-side, all right." Another threatened danger had thus turned out harmless to me; but this kind of incident was really far from agreeable; and as there seemed no probability that this claim would ever become an improved homestead; it was decided that I should move into the mining village two miles off.

So in the early autumn I bade farewell to the canvas house, and never saw it again. In town, we lived in a little frame cottage quite out of the crowd but near enough for protection. There were very few families, but two or three in the neighborhood, hearing my melodeon, soon formed the habit of dropping in, on certain evenings of each week, to "have a sing," as they expressed it. By and by, a clergyman living a few miles off called on us, and we arranged an appointment for him to preach in our sitting room, which was probably as large as any room in town, unless it were the bar-room of the tavern down in the ravine. He had appointments in several places; so could only come once in two weeks; but that might be an opening for something better in the future. Though we had been told there was, among the miners, considerable sport made of the "psalm singing" at our house; yet there was a good congregation gathered there—enough at least to crowd the room pretty well and tax the ingenuity of two or three to arrange seats for them.

It was interesting to any thoughtful person in those days to observe the bearing of many, among even the roughest miners, towards those who, they believed, were in earnest in religion. They seemed to watch such persons with a look of mingled curiosity and respect, and appeared very generally to consider it desirable to have some of that sort among them. But we had not an opportunity to hold many meetings there; for in the spring another removal was determined upon.

This time it was to one of the largest and pleasantest of the mining towns quite high up in the Sierra Nevada Mountains; higher than Weaverville, our first California dwelling place. Here we found ourselves at once in contact with a number of very good Christian people. There were three churches, all very well attended, and each sustaining a Sunday School. There was also a good sized public school, as well as one or two social and beneficent societies. Here I seemed to have found, in one sense at least, a rest. For a little more than twelve years we lived in that town, or so closely on its outskirts as to be always considered among its inhabitants. During that twelve years California passed through various periods of convulsion which seemed to threaten her welfare. Now it was the great Vigilance Committee-movement of San Francisco, which was felt to the very tops of the Sierras. Then the Frazer River excitement drained most of her towns of many inhabitants. Again, the Washoe fever sent thousands surging wildly over the high ridges they had once dreaded to approach; while at almost the same time the awful roar of Civil War burst from cannon on the Atlantic shore, and rolled over mountain and plain. For awhile it threatened to set every man's hand against his brother; and banish prosperity from our homes.

But after the storm there came a calm. Then the great Overland Rail Road became the theme of all

[139]

tongues, and in due time it helped to carry prosperity
to California as well as to the interior. And so life has
rolled on, not only for the twelve years of which I was
speaking, but for many years since. California as a
state has rallied from numerous shocks, and is now
smiling in prosperity; while her first adopted children
many of them, have passed away; and those remaining
have grown old, and look back on years of wonderful
experiences which they sometimes wish could be recorded along with the history of their adopted State;
for their children and their children's children to read,
that they might learn to love and reverence the God
who through all the devious paths of life ever guides
safely those who trust and obey Him.

Epilogue

Epilogue

I WAS born in 1855 in California. My native town
was a mining town in the Sierra Nevada—a place
five or six years older than myself. My earliest rec-
ollections include a very frequent wonder as to what my
elders meant when they said this was a new community.
I frequently looked at the vestiges left by the former
diggings of miners, saw that many pine logs were rot-
ten, and that a miner's grave was to be found in a lonely
place not far from my own house. Plainly men had lived
and died thereabouts. I dimly reflected that this sort of
life had apparently been going on ever since men dwelt
in that land. The logs and the graves looked old. The
sunsets were beautiful. The wide prospects when one
looked across the Sacramento Valley were impressive,
and had long interested the people of whose love for my
country I heard much. What was there then in this
place that ought to be called new, or for that matter,
crude? I wondered, and gradually came to feel that part
of my life's business was to find out what all this wonder
meant. My earliest teachers in philosophy were my
mother, whose private school, held for some years in
our own house, I attended, and my sisters, who were all
older than myself, and one of whom taught me to read.
In my home I heard the Bible very frequently read, and
very greatly enjoyed my mother's reading of Bible
stories. . . . Our home training in these respects was
not, as I now think, at all excessively strict. But without being aware of the fact, I was born a nonconform-
ist. The Bible stories fascinated me. The observance of

Sunday aroused from an early time a certain more or less passive resistance, which was stubborn, although seldom, I think, openly rebellious. . . . When I review this whole process [of education in an isolated family in a province where society was little more than a loose aggregation of individuals and the completion of that education in the midst of the closely-knit and powerful communities of Europe] I strongly feel that my deepest motives and problems have centered about the Idea of the Community, although this idea has only come gradually into my consciousness. This was what I was intensely feeling, in the days when my sisters and I looked across the Sacramento Valley, and wondered about the great world beyond our mountains.

JOSIAH ROYCE, *The Hope of the Great Community.*